D1349949

LIVERPOOL FIRSTS:
Great Merseyside Geniuses

Jack Cooper

Published by Sigma Leisure – an imprint of
Sigma Press, 1 South Oak Lane, Wilmslow, Cheshire SK9 6AR, England.

British Library Cataloguing in Publication Data
A CIP record for this book is available from the British Library.

ISBN: 1-85058-592-X

Typesetting and Design by: Sigma Press, Wilmslow, Cheshire.

Printed by: MFP Design & Print

Cover photographs: Main picture – Salthouse Dock and the "Three Graces" through the memorial arch for dockers killed in World War II (J.G. Cooper); smaller pictures, left to right – The Beatles plaque, Cavern Walks (Merseyside Photo Library); George Stephenson Heritage Plaque, Upper Parliament Street (J.G. Cooper); detail of the Liver Buildings, showing the Liver Clock and one of the two Liver birds (Merseyside Photo Library).

Preface

For some years now the inhabitants of God's Own Country, Liverpool, have been patiently suffering the slings and arrows of outrageous journalists from the national papers. To read their offerings, one could be forgiven for believing that our City had become a cross between Sodom and Gomorrah – in overdrive. Sadly, the press coverage has been largely negative and our image has suffered in consequence.

Those of us who, like myself, were born, bred, educated, employed and entertained here, have become sensitive to the forces that have shaped the minds and hearts of the people of the "Pool". We know it's an exciting and vibrant place to live; that the people have the proverbial hearts of gold; that our humour can be devastatingly funny, and, even more devastatingly, can cut the pompous down to size; and that no other place can rally round so effectively when disaster strikes. Remember Hillsborough? And the Blitz? Sadly, these are characteristics that others may not notice, or, if noticing, may not understand.

The primary object of this little volume, therefore, is to give my fellow Liverpudlians a chance to realise how much we have to be proud of. There has been, and there is still, a vast store of intelligence, inventiveness and cultural appreciation that has been responsible for a great number of innovations which have affected the kingdom, Europe and even the world.

The idea of producing a book dealing with Liverpool Firsts had been simmering for some years, and the collection of data started a long time ago. Then, on Radio Merseyside's *Billy Butler Show*, one morning in 1993, I took this as my theme, presenting some of the Firsts that had originated and germinated in and around "the Pool" and had later spread far and wide. The response from listeners was astonishing. There were a great number of phone calls and letters, all asking the same question, "Is there a book on Liverpool Firsts?"

There was clearly great interest so research began in earnest. As usual, Liverpool people have been most generous with their encouragement and information, and I take this opportunity of thanking them for their kind encouragement and for the help they have given via letters, books, cuttings, phone-calls and so on.

Perhaps the first "First" in this book should be Radio Merseyside's *Billy Butler Show* itself, featuring Billy Butler and Wally Scott (producer). Their good-humoured support for the production of this book is much appreciated.

As the *Billy Butler Show* had then the largest audience in the country for a local radio programme, it must be our first First. I am equally grateful to the encouragement and support of the "stars" of the Roger Phillips and Pauline Daniels Show on Wednesday mornings.

P.S. My congratulations to the shareholders of MANWEB and North West Gas who have made a killing on the light and heat I burnt during many a midnight hour. The least they can do to show their appreciation is to buy the book!

Acknowledgements

Many kind people on Merseyside have contributed in greater or lesser measure to the production of *Liverpool Firsts,* and to these good people I send my most sincere thanks for their courtesy in ringing or writing. I cannot acknowledge them all, but they understand that, I am sure. I think they will understand, too, the need for courtesy on my part in thanking, more specifically, those in Museums, Art Galleries, University Departments, Schools, places (and Palaces) of Commerce, and so on, who searched and thankfully found items of sometimes abstruse and often more general knowledge. There was never a refusal or a hesitation to have a look – but then, what else would you expect of Merseysiders, Liverpudlians or Scousers – or whatever category or name pleases you. The following is a fair sample of such helpful fellow-citizens. My sincere apologies to anybody omitted:

The Editors of the Liverpool *Daily Post* and the *Liverpool Echo* for allowing me to quote from the pages of these fine provincial Newspapers.

The Librarian and Staff of the Picton Reference Library who are the epitome of patience.

Adrian Jarvis at the Merseyside Maritime Museum.

The Librarian of the National Maritime Museum, Greenwich.

Colin Simpson at the Williamson Library, Birkenhead, especially for his assistance in choosing old plate photographs of Laird ships which are reproduced in these pages.

Alder Hey Children's Hospital, West Derby.

Mr Malcolm Guy, School of Tropical Medicine.

MerseyGuides: John Edwards, Anne Walton, Elizabeth Newell, Brian King, Val Hozack, Rita Cheesman, Mike Chitty, Fred Camenisch, Hilary Oxlade, Hilary Love and Bernadette Bynre.

Liverpool University: Dr David Edwards, Dr Mike Houlden and Dr Peter Rowlands, of the Physics Dept., Oliver Lodge Building, for their patient research on my behalf and for their many and humorous suggestions for improving the list of Firsts (e.g. "Get another author!")

Robin Tudor, Commercial Manager of Liverpool Airport (to thank him, "FLY LIVERPOOL!")

Mr A.D. Power, fellow West Derbeian, sometime co-author, local historian and friend.

Miss Janet Gnosspelius, Historian, Woolton.

Members of my two WEA "Liverpool Saga" classes. (Just to prove that a good teacher is always ready to learn from his pupils.).

Mr Arthur Townsend, MSc., fellow-graduate of the Class of '94 (the year, not our ages).

The Headmaster, Staff and Secretary, St Paul's & St Timothy's RC Junior School, West Derby, for their cheerful assistance in the duplication of material.

Mr Phil Young of the Merseyside Conference and Tourist Board.

Cammell-Laird's, Birkenhead, via the Librarian of the Williamson Library.

Maggi Morris, Faculty of Architecture, University of Liverpool.

Prof. John Ashton, Regional Manager, NHS Warrington.

Mr Knuckey, Marine Division, MD & HD (Seaforth).

Last, but by no means least, the *Billy Butler Show* – Billy, Wally and Co.- for their cheerful and helpful support, and to Radio Merseyside for allowing me free rein as regards publicising this book. Thank you all.

John G. Cooper.

In Memoriam

Early in 1994, one of our Senior MerseyGuides was taken from us. Her name was Anne Morton. She was a most professional Blue Badge Guide and a very kind person who was always ready to help us in our early days of Guiding. She was Chairman of the MerseyGuides Association for many years and a dedicated promoter of Liverpool and Merseyside. She has been deeply mourned and is greatly missed.

It transpired that Anne, too, was intending to write a book on Liverpool Firsts, but did not have time to realise her dream. So, the MerseyGuides thought it would be fitting for this little book to be dedicated to her memory.

In writing this dedication, it would not be out of place to send, once again, our sincere sympathies and assurances of respect and support to her husband, Roger, and the family. This I feel honoured to do.

John G. Cooper

Contents

FIRST THINGS FIRST!

The main problem in writing this book has been the arrangement of the great number of Liverpool Firsts into some useful order. The initial plan was to list everything in historical sequence and watch the growth of ideas from year to year. The only problem with such a system would be that the reader would have to keep referring back in order to see the relationship between a later First and an earlier First in the same category. The idea of an alphabetical list was also considered, but was rejected for the same reason. Eventually, it was decided to arrange items in related groups such as Health, Transport, Shipping, and so on. This would allow items to be arranged in historical order under each relevant heading. In addition, items are arranged alphabetically in the index.

The next problem was to decide in which category to slot items that tended to overlap categories – should all medical Firsts, for example, be listed under "Health" or "Liverpool University"? Some medical Firsts were produced by local doctors, while others were the result of university research. The obvious solution was to judge such items on their respective merits and categorize accordingly.

As regards the geographical scope of Firsts – whether to restrict Firsts to Liverpool only – it was decided not to be too rigid. Hence, the net has been spread fairly wide to include those places where new ideas were developed that had direct relevance to Liverpool's history. For example, Firsts on the Wirral have been included because of the ship-building, ferries, trams or the aids to navigation that were initiated there and which affected Liverpool, or were stimulated by Liverpool's very existence.

The next task was to determine what is meant by "Liverpool Firsts". First in the world, or in Europe, or in the UK or just the first time something occurred in Liverpool? Clearly, for the list to have any value, local Firsts – something that happened in Liverpool for the first time, but may have already existed elsewhere – would have to be discarded (except for something that might have special local importance or significance). So a priority established itself: first in the UK, first in Europe, first in the world.

It should be noted that words such as "longest", "highest", "largest" and "heaviest" all imply the quality of "First-ness". Similarly, a new book, sculpture, play, painting or a Nobel Prize is something created and therefore new in its field – a First. Note that all claims to be firsts are highlighted throughout the book in bold type.

As usual, any author worthy of the name makes a very simple act of humility before presenting the text of a factual work like this one – namely, that he is human and can therefore err (though he works desperately hard not to do so). If mistakes should occur, I would be the first to acknowledge my error and thank the reader for drawing my attention to it, for future correction.

As there are doubts about the claims of some items to be Firsts, it will not surprise the writer to finder a certain amount of controversy arising! So, please read on – and take pride in our Liverpool Firsts. Please remember that the great John Wesley thought highly of us: "The neatest town in England." We were first even then!

Abbreviations used in this book

D.P.:	Daily Post
HMS:	Her(His) Majesty's Ship
HRH:	Her(His) Royal Highness
IISNC:	Irish Inland Steam Navigation Company
IOMSPC:	Isle Of Man Steam Packet Company
L&MR (also LMR):	Liverpool Manchester Railway
LOR:	Liverpool Overhead Railway
LRO:	Liverpool Record Office
L&Y:	Lancashire and Yorkshire Railway
MD&HB:	Mersey Docks & Harbour Board
MD&HC:	Mersey Docks & Harbour Company (present title)
MMM:	Merseyside Maritime Museum
MV:	Motor Vessel
NMGM:	National Museums and Galleries on Merseyside
NWSIAH:	North Western Society for Industrial Archaeology and History
op cit:	book or work already mentioned or quoted
PHW:	Peter Howell Williams ("Liverpolitana")
P&O:	Pacific and Oriental line
RMS:	Royal Mail Steamer
RS:	The Royal Society
SS:	Steamship
THSLC:	Transactions of the Historical Society of Lancashire and Cheshire

ARCHITECTURE

Visitors to Liverpool have long been loud in their praise of the quantity and quality of the City's buildings, big and small. They are impressed when they learn, for instance, that there are more Georgian terraces, buildings and squares in Liverpool than in Bath, and they are even more impressed when shown the refurbishment that has been accomplished and is in process of being accomplished to restore this great architectural heritage.

Victorian

The buildings that first impress, of course, are the Victorian buildings which are on the grand scale – St George's Hall, William Brown Street, Castle Street and Albert Dock come readily to mind.

St George's Hall, opened in 1854, is claimed to be **the biggest and finest example of the Victorian classical revival in the world**, displaying both Greek and Roman influences. Designed by the 23-year-old Harvey Lonsdale Elmes (who died before his great work was completed) it is an extremely fine building, containing a grand Civic Hall (once used for banqueting and musical entertainment), two Law Courts, a Concert Hall, and **the largest organ in Europe when it was installed**. It housed the main Law Courts until

St George's Hall, ca. 1925

the opening of the new Law Courts by her Majesty, Queen Elizabeth II, in 1984, and was equipped with cells, retiring rooms (for the legal profession) and waiting rooms (for witnesses).

Galleries line the east and west sides of the Hall. They were often used as spectators' galleries when, for example, a great banquet was being held with a notable person like Charles Dickens giving an after-dinner speech or reading. The interior decoration is superb. As it is now open to the public for Guided Tours during the summer months, it would be pointless to provide any further description here. A visit, like a picture, is worth a thousand words – or more.

The Victorian classical buildings of William Brown Street (adjacent to St George's Hall) are an outstanding group. They include: the Museum and the Walker Art Gallery, which are second only to London in importance and visual impact; the Picton Library, whose rotunda is used, architecturally, to "turn the corner" in the street's building line; and the Quarter Sessions building at the top of the street. This fine panorama is looked down upon by the Wellington Monument which is strongly reminiscent of its Nelsonian counterpart in Trafalgar Square. Wellington's figure is made from the iron of French cannon captured at Waterloo. The neighbouring St John's Garden, with its fine collection of statuary honouring local men of note, completes a beautiful architectural vista. The Garden also contains a plaque commemorating the burial of **French prisoners of war (Napoleonic),** which is the only one of its kind in the country.

The true Liverpudlian may admit, reluctantly, that this group may be second to London, but he/she still regards it, at heart, as the finest in the world! Hence, these buildings are included in this collection.

Nelson Memorial

Nelson was the darling of the country after his many successes at sea, and cities vied with each other to provide a suitable memorial for its citizens to admire. The first effort in Liverpool was a total disaster, being simply a tall, tapering column reminiscent of Cleopatra's Needle. It was hastily taken down and re-erected in Springfield Park, which is alongside Alder Hey Hospital. It can be clearly seen from Prescot Road.

The second attempt was a great success and can be seen today behind the Town Hall in the middle of Exchange Flags. It depicts Victory placing the fourth crown of victory on Nelson's sword (Trafalgar, of course, after Copenhagen, the Nile and St Vincent). Nelson is seated, wearing a cloak, and from the side of the cloak, Death (in the form of a skeleton) has placed a bony hand on Nelson's left breast where, according to tradition, he was

Nelson's Monument with Derby House in background, 1906

shot by a French sniper's bullet. There is much more to see and ponder upon, and once again, a visit is urged on the reader.

The memorial was designed by Matthew Cotes Wyatt and cast by Richard Westmacott Jnr. The chief significance of this sculpture, apart from the Nelson story, is the fact that it was the **first public sculpture in Liverpool** (i.e. paid for out of public money).

Georgian Buildings

It is only in recent years that the public has really become aware of the immense heritage of Georgian buildings that Liverpool possesses. Obviously, all these edifices cannot be classified *en bloc* as Firsts, but several do possess much distinction and the following are taken as a sample.

The Town Hall

Begun in 1749 by John Wood the Elder of Bath, it suffered a serious fire in 1795 when considerable damage was done. James Wyatt (designer of the interior decoration of Westminster Abbey) was called in to assess the damage and draw up plans for repair and refurbishment. His design is the one to be seen today, incorporating some of the earlier Georgian building with his own ideas. Its claim to be a First? Well, no less a person than the Prince of Wales,

Castle Street in 1895 with the Town Hall in the background

son of Queen Victoria (and later King Edward VII), bestowed that accolade upon the building when he remarked that **the Reception Room in Liverpool Town Hall was second only to that in the Winter Palace at St Petersburg in Russia**. As he had spent much of his life enjoying hospitality in virtually all the major foreign cities he could well be considered an authority on the subject. Besides, the Royal opinion, presumably, surmounts all others, so who are we to cavil?

It, too, is now open for public inspection during the summer months, and again, the reader is recommended to see it rather than read about it. Blue Badge Guides are in attendance to show you round, and further details may be obtained from the Tourist Information Office in Albert Dock, or from the Welcome Centre in the Clayton Square precinct, or from the Town Hall.

St. George's, Everton

The story of St George's is both remarkable and entertaining. Remarkable because **the church is made entirely from cast iron,** which could be cast in a foundry in minutes, as opposed to the weeks or months required to fashion these features in stone or wood (the traditional method). It was an architectural and ecclesiastical revolution, both in design and in building material, but it was not well received by the ecclesiastical authorities because of the very revolutionary nature of its design.

The idea was the brain-child of John Cragg, 1767-1854, Liverpool iron-master and, in today's terms, a self-made millionaire. He had made a fortune in his Mersey Iron Foundry in Tithebarn Street. He was a promoter of the Liverpool Cotton Exchange (1803 – and the first in the country) and a founder member of the Liverpool Athenaum (No.12 on the register). He was described as, "A remarkable man to whom I cannot find a single gracious allusion on anybody's part!" (A.T. Brown, *How Gothic Came Back to Liverpool*, 1837.)

The second man was Thomas Rickman (1776-1841) who lived in the south of England for the earlier part of his life. He had tried a variety of occupations: assistant chemist, failed medical student (though he later practised medicine in Lewes, 1797), assistant grocer, employee in a London cornfactor's (1803-1807), his own business, and a declared bankrupt. He came to Liverpool and worked in an insurance firm (1808-1817). Later, he was appointed Head of Architecture at the Liverpool Academy, to replace the previous incumbent, Joseph Gandy, who had left Liverpool.

Rickman had one skill that was to prove useful – he was a fair hand as an artist, even to the extent of designing church buildings. He also made and painted 5,000 lead soldiers; **invented a book-keeping system;** later ran a thriving practice in architecture for the Church of England, his designs including New Court and St John's College, Cambridge; and **he coined the architectural term "Perpendicular".**

The two were introduced in 1812 and a partnership developed. Cragg wanted to try something new with his cast-iron, preferably ecclesiastical. Rickman possessed his own special skill in draughtsmanship which manifested itself in an urge to design churches (he already had one or two church designs on the drawing-board). The two men decided to construct a church on Everton Brow, alongside the site of the old beacon that had existed there from 1220 AD.

The parish was a wealthy one. Many businessmen, to escape the noisy and noisome atmosphere of Church Street and other streets in the rapidly-expanding port of Liverpool, had built their houses on Everton Brow to enjoy the fresh air and the marvellous view. Under the prime mover and principal landowner, Thomas Atherton (who was later to buy the land across the river and develop it into New Brighton), 110 shares were sold at £100 each at a meeting in the local coffee house. Pews were sold to the highest bidders among the original subscribers, and later resold so that profits were soon made on the original investment. Once profits exceeded expenditure, the gains were to be divided among the proprietors proportionally. The arrangement was approved in 1813 by Act of Parliament. Many seats/pews were "tied" to the proprietors and were sold with their property. It became an Everton joke that, "..a gentleman's best dividends came from St George's".

The dimensions are: length 119ft (40metres), width 47ft (15 metres), and height of tower 96ft (32 metres). The foundation stone was laid on 19th April 1813, it was consecrated by the Bishop of Chester on 26th October 1814 and the sale of pews in the coffee shop took place on 28th October 1814.

The architectural significance of St George's is twofold. Firstly, the standardised parts for the interior were made of cast iron (in Cragg's ironworks) and, secondly, the style of the design was unique in that it **marked the transition from the square design of the Georgian style to the Gothic Revival** re-introduction of " medieval processional linearity, with a high nave and low aisles, centred on the altar." (*The Iron Church*, R.F. Mould, 3rd edition, publ. 1983.) In other words, the design changed from a square shape, which did not focus on the altar, to an oblong shape with the altar at one end, thus centring attention on the altar.

Cragg and Rickman also built St Michael's-in-the-Hamlet, Aigburth – their second cast-iron church – and the five big houses comprising the hamlet, with Cragg's medievalism displaying itself in their names: the Friary (once Glebeland), Carfax (once known as the Nunnery), The Hermitage, The Cloisters and Hollymount. Hollymount, the odd one out in the medieval naming, was John Cragg's own residence. Pews in St Michael's were sold by public auction in a coffee house – the Toxteth Park Coffee House – on 30th June 1814. The foundation stone was also laid that year, and on Wednesday 21st June, 1815 (three days after the Battle of Waterloo) St Michael's was consecrated. The cost was £8,000.

St Michael's-in-the-Hamlet, the second cast-iron church, built in 1815

After the success of St Michael's and St George's, the English church authorities relaxed their original opposition to such a revolutionary church design and reluctantly gave it their blessing.

However, the inventiveness of the two men still had some way to run. Their next idea was the construction of enough cast-iron parts to make several small churches. These units were then crated-up and despatched by ship to the mission fields abroad. In today's parlance, **the first do-it-yourself church-building kit.** Apparently, many are still standing in rather more exotic settings than Liverpool's.

Despite this success story, the twist in the tail was that Rickman and Cragg got on together like oil and water. (Ref: *The Iron Church*, R.F. Mould, originally priced at £1. It is to be reprinted, in aid of church funds, and may be obtainable eventually at St George's. It is the finest value for money for a local history on the Liverpool side of the Mersey, containing details of Rickman and Cragg, the early parish, the church itself, and even some rousing tales of old Everton.)

Liverpool Cathedral

In the spirit of the New Testament story of the Marriage Feast of Cana, the Cathedral, like the good wine, has been kept until last for it is a truly magnificent building, dominating the townscape and thus fulfilling the prime aim of the early cathedral builders – to build to the glory of God.

Designed by the 22-year-old Roman Catholic, Giles Gilbert Scott (later Sir Giles), the building took 74 years to complete – 1904 to 1978. Her Majesty attended the Service of Thanksgiving and Dedication on 25th Oct 1978. The fabric is of local sandstone from the great quarry at Woolton, some five miles to the south-east of the Cathedral. The interior is beautifully furnished with marbles from many places in this country, enhanced by some very **fine stained-glass Gothic windows – the biggest in England.**

Once again, the reader is exhorted to visit. There are many accomplished Cathedral Guides there who are only too keen to show visitors the glories of this "last of the great cathedrals" (in Britain, at least), and the Cathedral Bookshop is probably the best-stocked with relevant literature in the county. One of the good handbooks available will provide the visitor with all the information on the Cathedral that could be absorbed in one visit, but the salient facts are summarised below:

¤ **The largest Anglican Cathedral in the World.**

¤ The world's fifth largest Cathedral.

¤ **The highest and heaviest peal of bells in the world.**

¤ **The highest Gothic arches in Britain.**

Liverpool Cathedral, from the Albert Dock, dominates the townscape

¤   **When installed, the largest organ in the world, with 10,690 pipes.**

¤   A tower 110 metres (331ft) high.

¤   **The highest vaulting in the world (58 metres (175ft) maximum).**

¤   The second longest Cathedral in the world (205 metres [619ft]).

(Ref: Liverpool Cathedral Official Handbook, 1924)

Metropolitan Cathedral of Christ the King

"If you want a cathedral we've got one to spare." (Line from a well-known local folk song, *In My Liverpool Home*.) To be precise, we have one-and-a-half to spare. This strange statement arises from the fact that under the Catholic Cathedral is a huge crypt, cut out of the massive local sandstone and containing some marvellous brickwork, which was all that was completed of an earlier design for the site. Work stopped on this site during WW2 – which spelt the end of a most ambitious plan to build, to the brilliant design of Sir Edwin Lutyens, a Catholic Cathedral that would have been higher than St Peter's in Rome and possibly the biggest in Europe.

The site, bought by the Archdiocese under the leadership of Archbishop Richard Downey, in 1930, was in a commanding position on one of the highest points in Liverpool, and was relatively cheap because it still contained the grim and forbidding buildings belonging to the old workhouse (the biggest in Europe in its day, with 5000 inmates). Sir Edward Lutyens

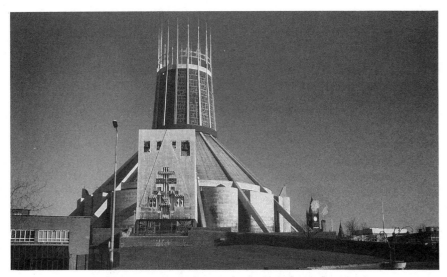

Liverpool Metropolitan Cathedral of Christ the King

came with excellent credentials – the Cenotaph in London and the Viceroy's House in New Delhi, India (seen in the film, *Jewel in the Crown*.)

The foundation stone was laid in 1933 and work began. By WW2, the crypt had been largely completed. After the war, in 1952, it was calculated that the estimated cost would be in excess of £27,000,000. Modifications were tried, but they would have made no significant difference to the ultimate cost. Archbishop Heenan was appointed and the decision was made to hold a design competition for a new design, incorporating the Lutyens Crypt. The winner was Sir Frederick Gibberd (1908-1984) who had designed London Airport buildings (Heathrow).

His design was revolutionary. It is a circular design with flying buttresses tapering up to the central lantern above the high altar. This lantern is crowned with slim spires, giving the crown effect called for by the Cathedral's title, Christ the King. Directly over the altar is another crown, in stainless steel, representing the Crown of Thorns. The dimensions of the cathedral are: height 78 metres, internal diameter 59 metres and seating capacity 2,200 people. The cost was £1,900,000 (subsequent interest rates inflated this considerably). It was opened by Cardinal Heenan in 1967.

The new Cathedral quickly achieved fame in two ways. It was one of six designs for a set of pictorial postage stamps depicting English Cathedrals, and it was even more rapidly awarded the loving nickname of "Paddy's Wigwam" by Liverpudlians of all denominations – a name derived from the shape of the building as well as a reference to the large Irish Catholic population in the city.

World's Largest Bonded Warehouse

1900: The Stanley Bonded Warehouse was opened for the safe storage of tobacco until duty had been paid and it had been cleared by Customs and Excise. It is a huge building, erected at one of Jesse Hartley's early docks, Stanley Dock. Massive castellated gates deter the would-be intruder by their forbidding bulk. When built, it was **the largest bonded warehouse in the world** (and may still be today).

The Stanley Dock itself was the raison d'etre of the Liverpool -Leeds Canal. Barges carrying intended cargoes from across Lancashire and Yorkshire dropped down the final fifty-five feet from the Canal into the dock via four locks. They were thus at the water level of the whole dock system. Today, thanks to Inland Waterways, the locks system has been preserved as an important piece of maritime and industrial archaeology, with lock gates still operable by hand. Attractive shrubs and trees complete a very pleasant set-up.

Jerry-Building

As a footnote to this section on Architecture it must surely be delightfully inappropriate to record that **the term "Jerry – built" is also a Liverpool First!** It derived from a firm called *Jerry Bros., Builders and Contractors* who, "..lived in Liverpool and built many of those rapidly constructed, ill-built and showy houses which formed so large a portion of this town and which were inhabited chiefly by the lower middle classes."

A Family of Streets

As a further footnote, one group of streets of ordinary houses deserves special mention. They are probably of much more concern to the people living there. This group can be found in Walton, near Everton FC's ground. The group is claimed as being unique in that **the initial letter of every street is taken from the names of the builders**, Owen and William Owen Ellis, who erected these houses, and the eldest son, E. Alfred (The "E" stands for "Elias".) The streets are arranged in name order and are as follows: Oxton, Wilmslow, Eton, Neston, Andrew, Nimrod, Dane, Wilburn, Ismay, Lind, Lowell, Index, Arnot, Makin, Olney, Weldon, Euston, Nixon, Liston, Imrie, Aston (all the foregoing are streets) and Stuart Road. E. Alfred is remembered in Espin, Askew, Linton, Frodsham, Ripon, Emery and Dyson. Research has not revealed any other group of streets named so originally and in such great number any-where in the country, so, a First it is!

ART AND ENTERTAINMENT

This section includes theatre, music, libraries, museums, poets, writers and anything that is even vaguely cultural (the reader is invited to decide what constitutes the "vaguely cultural". It often comes as a big surprise to outsiders to find that Liverpool people have a very high regard for their libraries, museums, art galleries, Philharmonic Hall, Playhouse, and "Empire" and are equally proud of the large number of such places of enlightenment and enjoyment to be found not only in the city but also in the suburbs. For instance, we possess four Carnegie Libraries, paid for from the profits of that remarkable Scotsman who made his fortune in America in railways and steel.

Ceramics

The Liverpool Pottery industry is not too well known – perhaps research into, and interest in, this branch of Art in the area are both comparatively recent. The Museum has a very fine collection of pottery of all kinds, including a fine display explaining the history of ceramics. If the reader is interested in this subject, he/she could do no better than visit the Ceramics Gallery in the Liverpool Museum in William Brown Street. The reader will find, for example, that there was a pottery on the site of the Museum itself and that another pottery existed on the site of Mothercare in the centre of the city (corner of Whitechapel and Lord Street).

Probably the best-known was the Herculaneum Pottery, 1796. The only reminder we have of this is the name, "Herculaneum", which was probably chosen because Josiah Wedgwood's Etruria Works (another ancient Italian name) had proved so successful in the Midlands. The name was used for the Herculaneum Dock, the Herculaneum Bridge Hotel and the Herculaneum Steel Fabrication Works. Sadly, the pottery lasted less than fifty years, but it may have earned a First for the fact that it had its own chapel and Sunday school.

The chief Liverpool contribution to the pottery industry was Sadler's discovery of how to transfer pictures on to pottery. (See: Sadler)

Libraries

The present trend of starving libraries of resources does not go down at all well in this great city where the first public libraries and lending libraries were founded. If our penny-pinching masters could visit the Picton Reference Library, for instance, any day of the week, they would find the place packed with people of all walks of life, busily researching families, Liverpool history, famous people, shipping, etc. Sadly, these resources are becoming badly worn with use and can only slowly be photo-copied or taped for preservation because of shortage of funding. It is possible that much source material will soon be lost forever.

1757: At the bottom of Bold Street stands the lovely Georgian *Lyceum*, designed by Thomas Harrison of Chester. It was built between 1800 and 1802 to house what is claimed to be **the first circulating library in Europe**, the Liverpool Library, founded in 1757. The nearest claims in other parts of the country are: Norwich, with the first public Lending Library in 1857; Canterbury, the first Municipal Lending Library, opened on 14th Jan 1847; and Manchester, the first Free Public Lending Library in the late 1850s (date not confirmed).

1823: Liverpool was the first town to have a **Mechanics Lending Library.** (D.P., 1969)

1850: Liverpool became **the first borough to have a library committee.** (D.P., 1969)

1860: Liverpool opened the **first, large, purpose-built library in Britain.** (D.P., 1969)

Music

The Beatles, The Fab Four, changed the course of musical history forever. Their originality, in music and style, shattered the contemporary scene, and their triumphs here, in the States, and elsewhere are now legend. How many Firsts can be credited to them is hard to assess, but here is a small selection.

1964: (4th April) The Beatles were **the first group to have the top 5 records in the American Billboard charts.** They also had 7 others in the top 100 at the same time.

1965: (26th October) **The first British pop group to receive MBEs.**

1967: (June) **First pop group to be seen simultaneously on TV by 4 million people** when *Our World* was beamed globally by satellite.

1967: *Sergeant Pepper* was **the first concept album** with no breaks between the tracks, each one led to the next from start to end.

1984: The first pop group to be given the freedom of Liverpool – although only Paul personally accepted it.

1988: Paul McCartney was **the first Western artist to record an album**

exclusively for the Soviet Union. It was called *CHOBA B CCP* (Trans: *Back to the Soviet Union*).

1989: (19th December) **For the first time in its 75 year history, the Performing Rights Society honoured an individual artist** – Paul McCartney.

1997: (March) **First Beatle to be knighted** – Paul McCartney.

(The writer is indebted to Blue Badge Guide and Beatle Guide Bernadette Byrne for the above.)

The Wurlitzer

It is not generally known that the Wurlitzer was the brain-child of a Birkenhead man, **Robert Hope Jones.** He had worked on organs for many years, then produced the idea of an organ played by remote control. During a trip to the USA, he went to the Wurlitzer Co., who got hold of the rights to his invention and marketed it as the Wurlitzer Organ. Jones had thereby lost the rights to, and credit for, his invention.

The Royal Liverpool Philharmonic Orchestra

The third oldest Philharmonic Society in the World, the Liverpool Philharmonic Society, was founded in 1840, as a Gentlemen's Club for Singing. It became **the first established Symphony Orchestra with its own Hall.** This first building burned down in 1933. The present building was opened in 1939, to the design of Liverpool architect Herbert Rowse. Apparently, his philosophy for the building was strongly influenced by the finding and opening of Tutankhamen's Tomb at that time. He designed the mezzanine to represent the outer tomb of Tutankhamen's last resting place, while the Auditorium was envisaged as the inner tomb with all its treasures. The decorations of both areas have an Egyptian flavour. These facts were on display on the mezzanine some years ago.

In 1957, the Philharmonic received the **"Royal" assent – the first orchestra to do so outside London.** After a two-year closure (1993-95) for essential repairs and alterations, the new "Phil.", as it is affectionately known, was re-opened in the Autumn of 1996 and surprised everybody. Thanks to an extra hard skin of concrete above the ceiling and behind the walls, the sound is crystal clear. It is now **claimed to be acoustically the finest orchestral hall in Europe.** Once again, the reader is urged to make a visit to look and listen, and thus appreciate its beauty. Innovation has been the key to the success of the Royal Philharmonic, considerably assisted by the Friends of the Phil. who have raised considerable amounts of money for the Orchestra.

Firsts for the orchestra include:

1901: The first perfomance of **Elgar's** *Pomp and Cicumstance March, No.1*, which was dedicated to the Phil by Elgar.

1944: The first public performance of *Bartok's Piano Concerto.*

1946: The first performance of **Britten's** *Young Person's Guide to the Orchestra.*

Post-WW2: The first to introduce **Industrial Concerts** – an idea later taken up by the London Philharmonic and the Hallé.

Post-WW2: The first to start regular *Musica Viva* series.

1969: The first **Seminar for British Conductors.**

1994: the Royal Liverpool Philharmonic was **the first orchestra to play underwater** on the occasion of the sixtieth year of the opening of the Birkemhead Tunnel (17th May 1994). The players actually sat on the boundary of Liverpool and Birkenhead inside the tunnel.

1995/96: each summer, while the hall was being refurbished, the Royal Liverpool Philharmonic ran a series of pop concerts, known as the Summer Pops Season, at the King's Dock. The main auditorium was a huge blue tent, attached to a smaller tent that allowed full "promenading" to take place. It was a brilliant idea, and because of its great popularity, it is destined to carry on every summer – even though the hall is fully refurbished and operational again! It was the UK's most successful **Summer Orchestral Festival,** with more than 25,000 people attending.

Two great names of the music world had long associations with the Phil – Sir Malcolm Sargent, who was Principal Conductor from 1942 to 1948, and Sir Adrian Boult (born in Liverpool in 1889, the son of an importer) who was **the youngest ever conductor** in 1916.

A large cinema screen emerges from the floor of the platform, and is fully utilised in presenting Classical Films. It has a big following. It was **the only such screen in England,** and only one other exists, in Leningrad. The screen, Proscenium and the machinery weigh some seven tons.

Diagonally across the road from the Phil stand the Philharmonic Dining Rooms, an Edwardian "gin palace", designed by Walter Thomas (the brewery architect), and built in 1900 to provide a room on the first floor for coachmen to enjoy a meal while awaiting their masters and mistresses at a Philharmonic Concert. It is a sumptuous building inside with its mahogany counters, crystal chandeliers, marble floors, copper panels, stained glass and carved plaster ceilings and dados. The outside is equally attractive with its stepped gables, oriel windows and attractive balconies. Above the Hardman Street entrances are carved reliefs of the great composers.

It is especially popular with coach parties touring the Liverpool Heritage Trail and their interest is further excited when they learn that the Philharmonic Dining Rooms possess **the finest Men's Victorian Toilets** in the country! To arrange for a coachload of visitors (of both sexes) to see this unique First for Liverpool requires a great deal of tact on the part of the Blue Badge Guide. It requires even greater forbearance on the part of the regulars who may have their own urgent need to visit this feature as a matter of immediate convenience.

Theatres

The *Playhouse Theatre*, Williamson Square is the **oldest Repertory Theatre in the country**. It was built in 1865 as the Star Music Hall, then reconstructed as a repertory theatre in 1911. Among the famous who have appeared there were: Rex Harrison, Noel Coward (his first ever stage appearance) and Gertrude Lawrence (both of whom appeared in a play here as children), C. Aubrey Smith, Cecil Parker, Michael Gough, and Diana Wynyard.

The *Theatre Royal* was **the largest theatre outside London** and was erected in 1772. It was closed in 1884, and it eventually became the Liverpool Cold Storage building in Williamson Square. It was demolished in the 1970s and a car park built on the site. Today, it is part of a vast rebuilding plan for this very central part of Liverpool. It was at the *Theatre Royal* that the actor Julius Brutus Booth played very successfully. His son, John Wilkes Booth, gained a much more notorious reputation, as the assassin of President Abraham Lincoln – an unwanted First for Liverpool.

1790: It was while visiting Liverpool, as a child, that William Hazlitt saw his first play, then wrote his **first drama criticism**. (D.P., 27th March 1969.)

1860s: A little-known theatre, the *Sans Pareil* in Manchester Street, was owned by Henry de Freece. He had the bright idea, in the 1860s, of introducing **twice-nightly performances**. The idea was later taken up by George E. Belmont in London.

1931: The locally famous Argyll Theatre, Birkenhead, opened in 1868 and lasted until 1940. It was **the first in Britain to broadcast a variety show**, on 14th April 1931. Over 100 wireless transmissions were made from the theatre, and in 1935, **it became the first music-hall in this country to broadcast direct to the United States**, on a coast-to-coast hook-up. (D.P., 21st August 1969.)

The Bluebell Girls

This famous dance troupe was founded in Paris by Margaret "Bluebell" Kelly of West Derby. She was born in Dublin, then brought to Liverpool from an orphanage by a West Derby nurse. She was nicknamed "Bluebell" by an Irish doctor because of her bright blue eyes. She grew up in West Derby, and because she had been slow to walk, dancing lessons were recommended by doctors at Alder Hey Hospital. After leaving St Paul's RC Junior School in West Derby, she went to Leyfield Convent. Aged 12, she made her stage debut as a pantomime babe at a Liverpool church hall. At 16, she left home to tour with the Alfred Jackson Girls.

At the age of 21, she founded the world's most famous dance troupe, in Paris – The Bluebell Girls. Her marriage to her Jewish husband, in France, led to some very fraught times indeed, for she had to hide him from the Gestapo on many occasions. A television serial of her life, some years ago, presented very vividly the trials and terrible dangers of hiding a Jew in Paris during the Nazi occupation. She is locally regarded with great esteem as a real heroine.

The Tatler

The first provincial Newstheatre, *The Tatler* was opened in Church Street in 1911. It later added Cartoons to its repertoire and became a most popular rendezvous for those requiring a short film show while, perhaps, waiting for a train or taking a break from shopping. The site is now occupied by Clarke's shoeshop. It was also the **first newstheatre to use Stereoscopic Films – 3D.**

A small cinema existed for a short time in Clayton Square, on the site of Sarah Clayton's house. It was called the *Jaycee* – presumably from the initials "J" and "C". Its presentations were a little more lurid than those at the Tatler. By a strange coincidence, when it closed down it was replaced by a Roman Catholic Chapel where the initials "J.C." had a more sober and meaningful significance. One Irish Catholic of the writer's acquaintance was heard to comment, with a knowing nod of the head, " The Divil hasn't got a prayer in Liverpool."

Another kind of Soap

The television soaps *Bread* (at the Dingle) and *Brookside* (at West Derby) have become nationally and internationally famous, but the seminal Soap was *Z-Cars* (set and filmed in Kirkby).

Liverpool Comedians

The list of Liverpool comedians must be well-nigh endless: Tommy Handley, Rob Wilton, Arthur Askey, Ted Ray, Ken Dodd, Jimmy Tarbuck, Tom O'Connor, Freddie Starr and Craig Charles. These are the better known ones, but there is a growing list of newer, younger comedians. **It would be safe to claim a First for the greatest number in the North, at least.**

Radio

Radio Merseyside, the third and largest of Britain's new local radio stations went on air at 12:30pm on 22nd November 1969. The first programmes had, literally, a mixed reception owing to transmission and link-up faults which distorted several programmes. Currently, it is the most popular local radio station, with **more listeners than any other local radio station in the country.**

Hollywood on the Mersey

Liverpool is the most filmed city in the UK, outside London. The city has doubled for many other cities such as St Petersburg, Dublin, Moscow and Venice. In addition, Bebington Oval was used for the outdoor shots for *Chariots of Fire*, while Bridge Cottage, in Port Sunlight Village, was used for indoor shots for the same film. Many films have been shot on location in and around Liverpool, including: *In the Name of the Father, The Hunt for Red October, The Titanic, Young Indiana Jones,* and *Letter to Brezhnev*.

BUSINESS & COMMERCE

The business world has attracted many uncomplimentary comments throughout history. Among many other unwanted detractions have been words such as: usury, sharp practice, avarice, inhuman treatment of workers, cartels, greed, bankruptcy, fraudulent trading, sweat shops and even industrial espionage. Like other things in life, we tend to base our judgements on the bad, the sensational and the wicked, whereas there is usually another side to the picture. For the populace to survive in a more or less prosperous condition, business must be carried on at many levels and in a highly competitive world / country / city ("market forces must prevail" has been the slogan of the Thatcherite years). Survival is very much the name of the game, and every businessman strives to gain that essential edge over other businessmen. To do so, there has to be inventiveness and innovation in all aspects of any business – the business policy, its buildings, communications, accounting systems, selling techniques, and so on.

The business world needs attractive premises, well-established public images (e.g. the famous Woolworth's slogan "3d and 6d Stores") and equally well-established virtues like reliability and fair trading (e.g. George Henry Lee's slogan "Never Knowingly Undersold".) Many businesses with worldwide reputations began here – **Meccano and Hornby Trains** are the most likely favourites of the writer's generation! These and others were clear Firsts.

Needless to say, throughout the last three centuries, Liverpool businessmen have been ahead of the game, often for long periods. The first tidal dock and the first enclosed dock system, for instance, are mentioned elsewhere. The contribution of our "letter of marque" ships and our privateers cannot be ignored for it was of the greatest value. It was they who shortened the sea-route to the Americas by sailing directly across the Atlantic to their destination, thus breaking with the traditional method of sailing – viz., southwards down the line of longitude until the latitude of, say, New York was reached, then westwards, along the line of latitude to that port. For readers who remember their geometry, the privateers sailed the hypotenuse of a right-angle triangle, while their competitors sailed the other two sides – a much greater distance. Sadly, we cannot claim a Liverpool First for this because we have no firm evidence, but it was certainly good business practice. Readers may care to believe that it was a First.

Pilkington's, St Helens

Pilkington's of St Helens opened their glassworks there in 1773. Up to 1870, they were **the largest privately-owned company** of any kind, and **the world's biggest glass-makers** with assets of over £100 million. Their greatest achievement was **the pioneering of the float glass process**, which made large sheets of glass (e.g. for shop windows) a possibility for the first time in history. The reader is recommended to visit the Pilkington Glass Museum at St Helens (admission free) to learn the full story in a very remarkable museum display.

Liverpool Underwriters' Association

The Liverpool Underwriters' Association is the oldest in existence, and was founded in 1803. In 1858, the Association was instrumental in raising £350,000 for the laying of the first Transatlantic Cable.

1841: The earliest known purpose-built and architect-designed office block was Brunswick Buildings, erected in 1841 – 42.

1843: The **Liverpool Victoria Friendly Society** established – the **biggest in the world in 1969.**

1850: The Liver Friendly Society established – from very humble beginnings.

1855: The first penny provincial newspaper in the country was begun in Liverpool.

1856: John Sadler was a famous Liverpool potter. The story is told of how he was clearing up after a watery playtime with his son when he noticed that a page of newsprint had dropped on to the wet floor. By the time he got round to picking it up, the paper had almost stuck to the floor.

He began to peel the paper from the floor and found, to his amazement, that the printed matter had been transferred to the floor covering. He realised at once the implications of this discovery – namely, that a picture could be transferred on to pottery the same way. He later worked with Wedgwood (who once worked in the Cloth Hall, opposite what is now Radio Merseyside) who brought his finished pottery to Liverpool for the new process of **transfer printing** to be applied to them. (A world First.)

Lewis's

Lewis's was founded by David Lewis in 1856 and became the flagship of the **first group of department stores to introduce central buying.** It opened purchasing headquarters in London so that it could better compete with the chain stores' **bulk buying – a practice which Lewis's had themselves pioneered** some time before. It was also **the first big store to be equipped**

with a sprinkler fire system – i.e. water sprinklers automatically came into play as soon as fire was detected. Unfortunately, during the 1941 Blitz on Liverpool, the building received a direct hit from a German bomb – right on the water tank on the roof. The building was badly damaged by fire.

Lewis's was always renowned for being ahead of the game when it came to new ideas. For instance, while the great steamship, the *Great Eastern*, was anchored off Cammell-Laird's shipyard waiting to be scrapped, its sides bore a white-painted sign in huge letters, **"BUY AT LEWIS'S STORES."**

The yearly Christmas Grotto at Lewis's was always a popular attraction, but perhaps one of their best advertising stunts occurred when a twin-engined, low-wing monoplane, ***Grosvenor House*, was lifted to the 5th or 6th Floor** (opposite the former Central Station) and put on display inside. It featured easy-access ramps so that children especially could climb up to see into the narrow, crammed cockpit that had been home for the two pilots, Scott and Black, while they broke the London to Cape Town flying record. Along with his youthful pals, the writer was enthralled to be able to look into an aeroplane cockpit for the first time – particularly because this plane had been occupying the headlines all through the record attempt.

Perhaps the name of the make of this plane was prophetic – the De Havilland *Comet*. **It was claimed that Lewis's was the first store to put on such a show.**

Oriel Chambers, Water Street

Oriel Chambers was designed by Peter Ellis in 1864, and was well ahead of its time. His design **improved the provision of natural light to the inner offices of the building. He used cast-iron framing throughout to support the floors, walls and roofing.** He made no attempt to conceal this cast-iron frame for the office windows are "hung" on the ends of the frames. Hence, the frontage on Water Street, for example, is almost entirely made of glass in bay-window form to allow maximum light into the offices. In more simplistic terms, the frontage should, by rights, fall down, being largely made of glass (see illustration). A Conservation Plaque, on the outside wall, draws attention to the innovative nature of the design. The glass overlooking the central courtyard is curtain walling with the glass passing in front of the iron building frame.

The technical brilliance of the building made a lasting impression on a young American named James Wellborn Root (1850-1891), who was regular visitor to Liverpool from his temporary home in Wallasey, around the time of the opening of Oriel Chambers. Born in Lumkin, Georgia, he was aged 11 at the outbreak of the American Civil War. His father, rightly concerned about the dangers in a country at war with itself, sent his son to the safety

Oriel Buildings, Water Street, designed by Peter Ellis, 1864

of a prosperous Liverpool which already had very strong American connections.

When Root returned to America, he became a partner in the architectural firm of Burnham and Root. This great Chicago practice designed many fine buildings in that city including the Monadnock Building – one of the best-known early skyscrapers. The building was distinguished by the vast amounts of glass used in its construction, to admit as much light as possible into the offices. Suffice it to say that Peter Ellis's work in Liverpool was exported to Chicago by a deep admirer.

Owen Owen's

In 1868, a 20-year-old Welshman of farming stock left his home village of Bwlch, near Machynlleth, with £300 in his pocket and came to Liverpool. He opened a shop in London Road, and opened an account with the North and South Wales Bank, with the confident assertion that he would achieve an annual turnover of £3,000. His name was Owen Owen, whose name and business are now part of the folklore of Liverpool The business closed as late as 1987.

The official history of the firm, *They Always Come Back* by Ian Hargreaves, relates how Owen started with a staff of two, and ended employing 6,000 people. **He pioneered the idea of a half-day holiday per week for staff and**

a five-day working week. The Owen Owen building in Clayton Square was originally planned as a luxury hotel, which may account for the comfortable ambience of the store in its heyday. There was a time when if an article requested was not in stock, a page boy would be sent out to purchase it elsewhere – even as far afield as Manchester!

Owen Owen had one strict rule regarding credit: "Give no credit to anyone for a longer period than two months – this can't be thought of at first." Up to the time of its closure, the firm had introduced such special credit facilities that "Owen Owen" had become the Welsh synonym for "on the never-never."

Liverpool Society of Chartered Accountants

Merseyside accountants were the first in England and Wales to band together as a professional body when, in 1870, they formed the Liverpool Society of Accountants. Ten years later, the Institute of Chartered Accountants was incorporated through the joint initiative of the Liverpool and London accountants. (D.P., 22nd July, 1969.)

Chadburn's

This famous Marine Engineering company obtained a Patent for a ship's telegraph in 1870. Very quickly their fame spread and their ships' telegraphs were soon being used by all the major steamship companies in the world.

NALGO

In 1896, a 26-year-old clerk in the Liverpool Town Clerk's department, by the name of Herbert Blain, established the **Liverpool Municipal Officers' Guild. It was the first association of local government employees in Britain to have membership open to everyone** from office boy upwards. When the idea became more widely known, **Blain founded the National Association of Local Government Officers in 1905. It is Britain's largest white collar union,** with 375,000 members in 1969.

General Accident Building

Opposite Barclays bank in Water Street is a unique building – the General Accident Building, which began life in 1899 as the head office of the Bank of Liverpool. Its uniqueness was accounted for by its **huge bronze doors,** each of which had a **sculpted tiger's head** (in bronze) of ferocious mien and wicked-looking teeth. The Lascars (Indian seamen who came from an area renowned for these man-eaters), as soon as they arrived in port, donned their best garb and, with their little shuffling run, reached the tigers as quickly as possible in order to stroke their teeth. Apparently, these two tigers' heads had a wide-ranging fame because it was considered good luck to stroke their teeth.

The site of the building was the birthplace of Major General Sir Banastre Tarleton, Bt, MP (1754-1833). He was a popular figure in Liverpool's history as well as being a national hero. He tried to put down the rebellion in America at the battles of Charleston, Philadelphia and New York, but was captured by George Washington at Yorktown in 1781.

1908: Tower Building (behind the present Liver Building) was among the **first steel-framed blocks** in the country and the first **in Lancashire.** Designed by W. Aubrey Thomas (18549-1934), it was faced with white faience tiles which allowed the rain to wash accumulated dirt off the building. It is on the site of the Tower of Liverpool, built and fortified by Sir John Stanley in 1406. The Stanley family later became the Earls of Derby.

1911: The Liver Building (1908-1911) was **the first multi-storey, reinforced concrete block of offices in the country**. Its design was based on a French invention, called Hennebique construction, whereby the building was built from the inside outwards by constructing an immense criss-cross framework of reinforced concrete. There was some influence from similarly designed buildings on the Chicago waterfront.

An undoubtedly valid claim for a First is made for **the Liver Clock faces** which **are the biggest in the kingdom**, being 2ft 6ins wider in diameter than Big Ben. Whether the famous Liver Birds are the biggest creatures in the country is not certain, but they are taller than a double-decker bus, being 6 metres (18ft) in height (see cover). Local tradition has it that they are of different sexes: the female bird faces the river to await the sailors coming off the ships (an echo of the famous Maggie Mae legend, perhaps) while the male bird, it is claimed, faces inland to see if the pubs are open in Liverpool!

The very pleasant chimes of the Liver Clock are not the result of chiming bells, but of stretched piano wires being struck by beaters – like piano hammers striking the piano strings. The sound is greatly amplified by amplifiers positioned just under the Liver Birds on the clock tower. Called Great George, the Liver Clock was started at exactly the moment that King George V was crowned in Westminster Abbey – a feat worth recording as a First in itself because **it was accomplished via an open telephone link with an observer at Westminster.**

Liverpool Trade Protection Society

Founded in 1923, the Liverpool Trade Protection Society was **the first mutual assistance organisation in England**. It was better known as a debt collecting agency. It existed for, "The protection of tradesmen, by the exposure of persons obtaining goods in a fraudulent manner."

It was formed as a guardian of trade – viz, for the Protection of Trade Against Swindlers and Sharpers.

Johnson Brothers, Bootle

In 1971, Johnson Bros (Johnson's the Dyers, as they were known locally) was celebrating its 151st birthday. They were known as **the biggest cleaners and dyers in the world**. They were formed in 1820.

"Whisky Galore"

The film "Whisky Galore" was wonderful entertainment, based on one of Compton Mackenzie's delightful novels set in the Hebrides. The ship, which was wrecked during a storm with its priceless cargo of whisky aboard, was the *Politician*. **The real-life ship was insured by a Liverpool firm.** The Average Adjuster (an important official of the insurance company involved) worked for the Liverpool firm of C. Danson & Co.

Barclays Bank, Water Street

This was another pioneering building of advanced design by Liverpool architect, Herbert J. Rowse (1887-1963). It was originally built in 1932 as the Head Office of Martin's Bank. It was well ahead of its time, with special features like **completely ducted cables and pipes, and low-temperature ceiling heating.** It remains a most impressive and beautiful building – especially the ground floor banking area. After the fall of France in WW2, 1700 boxes of gold were stored in the basement, awaiting shipment to Canada. The gold was a large part of the country's gold reserves and would have been used, in the event of a German of invasion of England, to carry on the fight against Germany.

Woolworth's

1909: Britain's and Europe's first Woolworth's Store was opened at 25-25A Church Street, Liverpool, in 1909 by Frank Winfield Woolworth (the site is next-door-but-two to the old Tatler News Theatre). The site is now occupied by Clarke's shoe shop. If the reader cares to stand outside C & A and look up at the end gable of the present Clarke's, he/she may just discern the faint markings that were left after recent repairs were effected. The following words are barely discernible: "F.W. WOOLWORTH. 3d and 6d STORES." Woolworth's third store in Britain was opened in London Road a short time afterwards.

In 1923, when the old St Peter's Church was demolished, Woolworth's built their large and better-known store on the site. If the reader looks carefully at the top of this building (which is still standing even though Woolworth's have moved out) he/she will see the Crossed Keys of St Peter. On the pavement in front of the store there is still a grey-green granite slab, with a brass Maltese Cross impressed into it, marking the site of the door of the old Church.

Match-making

Bryant and Mays are probably the best-known match-makers on Merseyside. They were equipped with **the first continuous match-making machine** in their Diamond Factory.

Hornby Trains, Meccano Sets and Dinky Toys

As far as the writer's and his contemporaries' childhoods are concerned, the most pleasurable memory of that golden age of the late twenties and the thirties is the possession of **a Hornby Train, a Meccano Set and "Dinkies" (Dinky Toys).** There can be no way of computing the hours spent building cranes, ships, planes, windmills and roundabouts and a host of models. The appeal, particularly of Meccano, was deep, calling on one's inventiveness, patience, planning ability, manual dexterity and a great number of other skills which gave great mental and emotional satisfaction when a particular model was constructed – and worked!

The inventor of these fabulous toys with their international appeal was Frank Hornby, of Liverpool, 1863-1937, who had two small factories. His second factory was in James's Street, next door to the Underground station, and the third in Binns Road, Wavertree – the home of Meccano and Hornby. Memories are made of this!

There is yet another satisfaction enjoyed by those of us who have kept our Hornbys and Meccano and Dinkies in reasonable condition – they are now quite valuable – a sound investment we did not even know we were making! Three Firsts for Frank Hornby, undoubtedly.

Power of the Municipality to Buy and Sell Land

1936: Liverpool was the first municipality to obtain powers by Act of Parliament to buy and sell land for industrial purposes, to erect factories, and to lease, sell or advance mortgages on such property. The date was 1936, and it was well ahead of the Hunt Report which eventually led to such powers being made statutory for the whole country. The outcome was the creation of industrial estates at Speke (140 hectares, 340 acres) and Aintree (120 hectares, 300 acres) after the allocation of land for industrial development. (D.P., 28th August 1969.)

United Voluntary Organisations

The calls on our pockets and purses for charitable purposes is endless. Liverpool people have an unequalled reputation for giving generously and promptly, and many institutions have benefited greatly – e.g. Alder Hey Hospital and Clatterbridge Hospital. We are proud of this facet of our life-style – perhaps because "the past is too much with us". It was this spirit that prompted the formation, in 1953, of the United Voluntary Organisations – a consortium of local societies which raised money for distribution to various charities. The idea of the scheme was brilliant in its simplicity: employees of Merseyside firms voluntarily had a set amount of their weekly wage or salary deducted at source. The scheme realised £25,000 in 1953, which was distributed to more than 40 charities.

Windowless Factory

The first windowless factory was opened at the Kirkby plant of Kraft Foods in 1957.

Barker and Dobson's

Barker and Dobson's were **the first sweet manufacturers in the country to provide boiled sweets with wrappers.**

Drive-in Bank

1959: The first drive-in bank in Britain was the Prince's Road branch of the Westminster Bank, opened in 1959. Just to emphasise Liverpool's lead in this branch of business, Liverpool's Martin's Bank later opened the first drive-in bank in the centre of a city – the city of Leicester. (D.P., 10th April 1969.)

The World's Shortest-Lived Bank?

The *Daily Post* (12th March 1969) carried an unusual letter headed, "The Bank with the Short Life Expectation". The text is reprinted here, and adequately displays its own feeling of astonishment.

"Liverpool's most unusual bank is scheduled to open on March 31. It is out of the ordinary because it's taken only five to six months to build - yet it will be one of the biggest in the city. And after a couple of years or so, it will close its doors, never to open again.

In Moorfields, it is to be the temporary home for the Dale Street branch of the Midland – one of the Company's two biggest branches in Liverpool. The other is in Castle Street, and it is a toss-up which is the larger. The temporary bank is to have an amenity to be found at no other central city bank I know . . . its own car park for customers." (First and last, perhaps?)

The Friendly Doors

The doors of the Co-operative Bank in Castle Street (1892) must surely be unique, locally and world-wide. They were designed and sculpted in bronze by the Victorian sculptor, Stirling Lee, who designed the building. The door panels are most attractive, and were designed for the first bank on the site, the Adelphi Bank, which lasted but 37 years, before being acquired by the Lancashire and Yorkshire Bank about 1899. This was later absorbed by Martin's Bank in 1928.

The panels depict three pairs of friends and one pair of brothers to illustrate the Adelphi of the bank's name: David and Jonathan, Roland and Oliver, Achilles and Patrochlus, and Castor and Pollux (the "Heavenly Twins"). The last named, of course, can be seen in the night sky in the constellation *Gemini*, and were familiar to RAF Navigators in WW2.

Insurance

The Prudential Building, in the familiar blood-red brick of its designer "Slaughterhouse" Waterhouse (See: Liverpool University) stands in Dale Street. Completed in 1886, the building is **the only major Gothic commercial building in Liverpool**. It is a scaled-down version of that Company's much grander building in High Holborn, London, which is so reminiscent of the Chateau Frontenac in Canada. The statue of St Prudentia is said to be a creation of Waterhouse's imagination.

Round the corner, in Castle Street, is another distinguished building dealing with insurance – the British and Foreign Marine Insurance Company building. It is in red brick and stone, with attractive mosaic panels depicting the history of cargo ships from dhows and triremes, via sailing ships, to steam vessels. It contains almost every type of architectural decoration, in the architectural handbook with swags, paterae, etc.

The British Workman Public House Company

1875: This was a venture thought up by the Temperance movement. **The first "pub" was opened in 1875, selling cocoa, coffee, tea and light refreshments.** Previously, dockers could only get food on the Dock Road from licensed premises. Within a few years there were eighty British Workman Public Houses (in effect, cocoa rooms) as the movement spread throughout the UK.

1963: The **Merseyside Council on Alcoholism was established** – the first regional office of the National Council on Alcoholism. It was the model for many more established in London, Zambia, etc.

The Lady Lever Art Gallery, Port Sunlight

Vauxhall Motors

The Vauxhall Motors car plant was the **first automatic one in the world to gain the BS (British Standard) 7750 for environmental management systems.**

Computers

1960: Martin's Bank, Liverpool, was **the first bank in the country to use a computer** – it coped with 30,000 accounts in five hours.

1962: The Mersey Docks and Harbour Board became **the first port authority in Britain to install a computer.**

Also Founded on Merseyside

Unilever was founded by William Lever after the great success of his new Sunlight Soap Works at Port Sunlight. **Port Sunlight Village,** which he helped to design and build, **was the leading industrial village in the country.** Hartley's Village, Price's Village and Cadbury's Bourneville have either faded away or have extended their original boundaries. Port Sunlight has not changed.

Football Pools are synonymous with Liverpool– Littlewoods and Vernons both started (and stayed) here.

COMMODITIES

Sugar

1872: The date of the opening of Tate and Lyle's sugar refinery in Love Lane is generally accepted as 1872, though no definite date can be assigned because documentation does not seem to exist to prove a date. It was built alongside the Liverpool-Leeds Canal, near the latter's terminus at Leeds Street in Liverpool. It was the **biggest sugar cane refinery in Britain**, eventually joining forces with MacFie and Sons, George Jager and Co., the Merton Grove Co., and United Molasses. The last-named broke away in 1957.

Sadly, for it was a big employer of labour, Tate and Lyle's closed down on 22nd April 1981, though staff left on or before 30th April 1982. Today, there is not a single relic remaining of the vast site once occupied by this great firm. It is not generally known that Henry Tate began his sugar refining business in a big warehouse-style building in Manesty's Lane (behind the studios of Radio Merseyside) which stretched from Hanover Street (Duke St. end) to Church Street. (Later, a big store, C & A Modes, was built at the Church Street end, so Manesty's Lane ends, today, at School Lane.)

The reason for the reduction of the plant, and its eventual closure, was the discovery by Margraf, in 1747, that sucrose could be extracted from the humble beetroot. The first attempt to produce sugar from beet was by Archard, at a place called Cunern in Silesia, in the early 19th century. In 1813, Napoleon gave a major boost to sugar beet production when he decreed that the import of sugar into France was banned because it came from British colonies and was, therefore, contraband and unpatriotic material.

(A full description of the foundation, growth and processes of the Love Lane Refinery can be found in *The End of a Liverpool Landmark* (1985), by J.A. Watson, who also wrote *A Hundred Years of Sugar Refining* (1973), both published by Tate and Lyle Refineries.)

Corn Exchange

The abolition of the East India Company's monopoly of the India Trade in 1813 and the China Trade in 1833 gave a great fillip to Liverpool's fortunes. New oceans were opened up to local merchants, which helped the city to prosper. This led to the erection of some fine buildings – India Buildings, Exchange Buildings, the Cotton Exchange (see below) and the Corn Exchange.

Corn has been the most vital commodity throughout history, not only in its essential value as a food source, but because of the power it gave to our lords and masters. Those who controlled the corn supply – e.g. via the King's Mills in Norman and medieval times – controlled the people. Tolls were imposed from the start of Liverpool's history, and it was not until 1755, as a result of the opening of the new Town Hall, that the Mayor and Bailiffs gave up all claim to the corn tolls – in exchange for increased Annual Fair dinners for which they were voted 120 guineas. (If this figure is multiplied by 200 to bring it up to present-day values, it would be the equivalent of over £24,000 – a very sharp deal indeed for the mayoral "mess of potage.")

With the opening up of trans-ocean trade, corn came high on the import list. In 1808 the first Corn Exchange was built, at the corner of Fenwick Street and Brunswick Street. By 1927, next to Minneapolis, Liverpool was the largest flour-milling centre in the world, with over 700,000 tons of wheat milled. It was inevitable that special marketing arrangements would have to be made – hence, **the Corn Exchange**, the **only one in England**. The first Corn Exchange was destroyed by enemy bombing in WW2. The foundation stone of the present building (which can be seen to the right of the Fenwick Street entrance) tells us that it was laid by Lord Woolton on 19th July 1953 (by a strange coincidence, the date, 43 years later, that this entry is being made!).

Incidentally, it was a Liverpool corn merchant, Joseph Sandars, who was instrumental in bringing the **Liverpool to Manchester Railway** into existence. He had heard of the steam railway experiments in Northumberland, around 1820, and made it his business to visit Killingworth Colliery where he saw steam locomotives in action. He met George Stephenson and saw the Stockton and Darlington Railway under construction. When he returned to Liverpool to tell local merchants what he had seen, there was a favourable response and no difficulty in finding investment and support. (See: Railways)

Cotton Exchange

1906: From 1820 to 1860, Liverpool handled at least 80 per cent of raw cotton imported into the UK. Perhaps the reader may care to work out what that percentage meant in bales of cotton from the import figures for cotton into the UK during the same period – namely, 700,000 – 800,000 bales.(Ref: P. Aughton, *Liverpool: A People's History.*)

Liverpool's Cotton Exchange was **the first in England** because we were the main cotton importing centre. It was built in 1906, between Ormond Street and Edmund Street (off Old Hall Street), for the Liverpool Cotton Market which, up to the outbreak of WW2, was one of the most important commodity markets in the world. Sadly, the contraction of the cotton trade and the reorganisation of Lancashire's textile industry, in the face of intense (some would say, fatal) opposition from the Far East, rendered the Cotton Exchange obsolete. The Cotton Association sold it to developers who demolished the imposing facade and replaced it with a tower office block. Architecturally, it was a poor exchange for what had been there before. The old facade was a beautiful and imposing sight, and its passing is a sad loss to our heritage.

Some idea of the size of the old facade can be gleaned from the stone figures – badly eroded by Liverpool's acid atmosphere – which stand on the pavement in Old Hall Street and in the courtyard. These figures originally stood on top of the towers of the old building, and depicted Science, Industry and Commerce. The courtyard also contains the very fine Cotton Association's War Memorial (WW1) – a bronze figure of a British "Tommy" in full battle kit, by the sculptor, Francis Derwent Wood, R.A.

HEALTH

If you neglect your health, you die. That is an inescapable fact of life, so mankind has been greatly concerned with health throughout history. The Bible, for instance, detailed the requirements for maintaining the health of the great number of Jewish migrants as they sought their Holy Land (Books of Exodus and Leviticus), medical research is said to have originated in the Middle East, the Chinese gave acupuncture to the world, and the Greeks and Romans were almost paranoid about their physical and mental condition. Their motto "Mens sana in sano corpore" (usually translated as, "a healthy mind in a healthy body") became the educational tenet of English Public Schools.

Medieval history reveals how rife was the dabbling in matters of health by all kinds of untrained quacks, mountebanks, witches and even the humble barber. The last-named not only attended to matters hirsute but bled people with leeches and even undertook surgery – which is the reason for the barber's pole being painted red and white.

Certainly, in a seaport like Liverpool, health (or lack of it) presented serious problems due to the diseases brought in by sailors from foreign shores. Eventually, concern about the health of sailors at sea deepened so that, in time, the ship's surgeon became an essential member of the crew. Right up to the present day, there are many doctors who gained valuable medical experience by acting as ships' doctors before they went into practice ashore.

Liverpool, however, had its own special problems regarding health. The port was, in 1840, "the unhealthiest port in western Europe " according to one source. The primary cause of the problem was the Industrial Revolution which had created high concentrations of industry and population in the rapidly growing manufacturing areas (Birmingham, Manchester, Liverpool, etc.), but without provision of the necessary health and sanitation services. The City's future Medical Officer of Health wrote, in 1842, "Whole districts are as plagued as the cholera smitten cities of India."

Vauxhall (Liverpool), in the mid-1800s, had a population of 142,000 people per square mile when the average for Europe was some 25,000 per square mile. We currently pride ourselves on the number and quality of our Georgian terraces, squares, houses, and so on, but it should also be borne in mind that it was the Georgian "developers", from the south, who also built our Georgian slums. These were characterised by cramped courts, unhealthy environment, poor sanitation, no running water, and coal-fired hearths pumping out reeking and carcinogenic fumes (for those who could afford the coal). The average expectation of life was 17 years of age, and slum

Back-to-back housing at the top end of Seel Street, on the right

houses usually accommodated one family per room. It is against this grim background that we have to look at the development of health services, and our record is a proud one.

The sick, like the poor, have always been with us, but their treatment has tended to be cursory and even dependent upon the whims of social esteem, status or local politics, or a combination of all three. Yet there were stirrings of social conscience among the more leisured classes. They had the time to think and plan, and the wealth with which to bring plans to fruition – providing there was also the will. The following list summarises the achievements in improving health by both the leisured and the not-so-leisured.

1679: The first **Seamen's Charity in England was opened.** With the proceeds, almshouses were built on the south side of Dale Street, near the Old Haymarket (now marked by the approach roads and entrance to the Queensway Tunnel). Other ports later followed suit.

1692: Silvester Richmond (referred to as the father of the Medical Profession in Liverpool) gave £100 towards the building of almshouses on the south side of Shaw's Brow (approximately the site of the present St George's Hall).

1736 -1779: 35 provincial hospitals were created, thanks to local effort and involvement. Liverpool was one of the first to act. It can truly be said that "our 18th century forefathers initiated the voluntary hospital movement". (Bickerton, T.H., *A Medical History of Liverpool from Earliest Days to the year 1920.* LRO)

1745: On the "Oyl Mill Field", on Shaw's Brow, the building of the **Infirmary commenced on the 3rd April 1745.** The reader will no doubt appreciate the significance of the date – the second Jacobite rebellion (the '45) – which delayed work on the new building. It was not finished until 1748, and was opened on 25th March 1749 by Edward, 11th Earl of Derby. The building cost £2,618 (to be multiplied by 200 to give an idea of today's value), and the first patients entered in 1749. (Bickerton: *op cit.*) First in the North of England.

Edward Rushton's pioneer work to create the first School for the Blind began about this time, and is described below.

1749: A local Act was passed for the cleaning of streets, long before Parliament approved a similar Act for the whole nation. Liverpool led yet again.

1752: A hospital for "decayed" seamen was built. It was supported by the monthly contribution of six pence (6d) by every seaman in Liverpool. (6d is approximately £6 50pence at today's value.) Other towns later followed suit.

Sugar Diabetes

1776: Diabetes has been with us a long time and is referred to in ancient books on medicine. It was Dr Matthew Dobson, a Liverpool physician living in Harrington Street who, in 1776, tested and found sugar in the urine of diabetics, and so **discovered sugar diabetes** *(diabetis melitis)*, which he defined as "the failure of the body to assimilate sugar".

He also demonstrated that **body temperature is virtually constant and unaffected by environment** – in other words, the body has its own temperature control system. We know this now, but Dobson pioneered the research, so, a legitimate First.

His practice was taken over by Dr Joseph Brandreth who pioneered the cold water treatment of fever. He was a native of Ormskirk where a hospital was later named after him.

First Dispensary

1778: The poor still needed help in obtaining medicines and drugs, so the **first dispensary was opened** on 31st August 1778 in a small rented house at 25, Princes Street, but the demand was so great that a bigger dispensary had to be opened on Church Street in 1781, at the corner of what is now Post Office Place.

Mentally Sick

1792: Due almost entirely to the great public-spirit and energy of Dr James Currie, the attention of the town was turned towards the mentally sick. The usual treatment had been one of horrifying indifference or consignment to a gaol to contain the sometimes frightening behaviour of the lunatic. Even the very name showed the thinking of the day – "an affliction due to the moon's influence" – and there was even ecclesiastical pronouncement of mental illness, being assigned the status of "the will of God". It was against this background of ignorance or indifference or inconvenience (or all three) that Currie began his fight for the care of the mentally sick and their proper and prompt treatment.

There was bitter opposition to his plea to erect a special building near the Infirmary in which to create the quietness and calm needed in treating this difficult condition. One can easily imagine the typical reactionary comments of an unfeeling Town Council, but Currie pursued his ambition. Eventually, an Asylum was proposed in 1789, and Liverpool **Lunatic Asylum was opened in 1792** in the Infirmary Garden. It was not a wholly popular decision.

1796: Currie was the first to use **hydrotherapy** for the treatment of fevers (Ref: *Medical Source Book* at Liverpool University.)

For a full grasp of the awful conditions existing, and of the total commitment of men like Silvester Richmond, the reader is recommended to read Bickerton's book, *op cit*, in the LRO.

First Woman Doctor

One or two sources claimed that the first fully qualified woman doctor to open a practice in Britain did so in Liverpool in 1886, but there seems to be no evidence to support this claim. The *Shell Book of Firsts* states that the first qualified woman physician in Great Britain was Elizabeth Garrett Anderson, daughter of a Whitechapel (London) pawnbroker. Her ambition to become a physician was inspired when, in 1859, she met Dr Elizabeth Blackwell, the American who became the first woman doctor in the world. She achieved this only after a terribly long and hard fight against the forces of male chauvinism, ingrained conservatism, blind stubbornness and total opposition to change – which seemed to be the accepted virtues of the age.

There have been claims that some women, although unqualified, actually practised medicine, including Mrs Bootle (of Peele, Cheshire) and Widow Bolton, both of whom attended to Nicholas Blundell's family at Crosby Hall (blood-letting was quoted in the Blundell diaries as being practised by these good ladies), and also a Mrs Maginis. Neither confirmation nor refutation has been found of these claims, which makes them of doubtful value as Firsts in medicine. (A very full account of Drs Blackwell and Garrett, and of their fight to win through, can be found on page 202 of the *Shell Book of Firsts*.)

School for the Blind

Edward Rushton (born 1772) was a seaman who worked on the slave ships in the late 1700s. He was clearly a man of deep feeling and sensitivity because on every ship on which he served, he insisted on entering the hold where the black slaves were kept, in order to comfort them. Unfortunately, some were stricken with a particularly nasty disease called malignant ophthalmia (probably trachoma – a common cause of blindness in developing countries, according to a member of the medical profession). He caught the disease and became blind himself.

When he returned home, he was turned out of his home by his stepmother (probably through fear of contracting the disease). He set about forming a school for the blind, recruiting support wherever he could, and there was soon enough financial help to open the first premises at 6, Commutation Row, Islington, opposite the potteries on Shaw's Brow, in

1791 – **Britain's First School for the Blind**. The School soon had to be transferred (1800) to bigger premises on the south side of London Road because of the demand (on the site of the Odeon Cinema, London Road). Liverpool was well ahead of any other town in the country, as a list on page 49 of *Pioneers and Perseverance* by Michael W. Royden, shows.

About the same time, **Liverpool forced through a law which decreed that every slave ship should carry a surgeon**. Sadly, this law quickly became abused. The title "surgeon" became a euphemism for anybody carrying a certificate of apprenticeship in medicine. This was hardly surprising, considering the grim conditions for surgery or treatment on board a slave ship.

1851: The London and North Western Railway Company (LNWR) was instrumental in forcing the school to move, yet again, to new premises. The enlargement of Lime Street Station (built 1836) was pushed through, which meant the end of the Blind School and its Chapel. On 6th April 1847, the Chaplain was authorised to conclude an agreement with the LNWR to build a School and Chapel on LNWR land at the corner of Hope Street and Hardman Street. The deal was finally agreed in August 1849. (*op cit*, p.124).

1850: July. Work completed.

1851: 11th July. 85 pupils began their school life in the new building.

1893: The Elementary Education (Blind and Deaf Children) Act led to the Hardman Street School for the Blind having to move out to Wavertree (the present site) in 1898, for children aged 8 to 16.

1859: Another attempt to help the blind was made in Cornwallis Street where the Liverpool Workshops for the Blind were sited. By 1861, there was not enough room there, so the people from the Workshops moved into the Hardman Street building after alterations had been made.(*op cit* p.150).

1932: 31st October. A new extension to the Hardman Street building was opened by Lord Derby.

Reliefs round the top of the building illustrate the activities undertaken by blind people at the school. The yard at the rear (approached from Hardman St) is worth seeing to gain some idea of the setting and atmosphere of the original School.(*op cit* p.176)

1966: The school received the Royal assent and became the Royal Liverpool School for the Blind. It stands in Church Road, Wavertree, opposite Earle Football Ground which is next to the old Abbey Cinema site.

However, this is a story with a happy ending (for Rushton, at least). He became a well-known poet, wrote hymns, opposed the slave trade, became a newspaper editor, bookseller and tavern-keeper and regained his sight following an operation. (D.P. 25th February 1969, LRO.)

Blindness in the Newly-Born

The first person to discover that venereal disease in a parent caused blindness in a new-born baby *(ophthalnia neonatorum)* was Arthur Nimmo Walker. He applied his findings, with notable success, at St Paul's Eye Hospital, Old Hall Street, in 1908.

Guide Dogs for the Blind

Guide Dogs have a very warm place in the hearts of anybody of feeling. Appeals for the provision of them and television programmes about their training and value are frequent, and (in the case of the appeals) well supported. It was not always so. **Britain's first Training Centre for Guide Dogs was opened in Wallasey in 1931.** One of the first local reactions was a summons, following complaints by local residents who were annoyed by the constant barking of the dogs. The case was lost "on a technicality" according to the *Daily Post* (1st April 1969). There is now a Guide Dog Training Centre next to Christopher Grange, West Derby, which has been opened for over a year.

Children's Health

Praise is due to the great Victorian writer, Charles Dickens, who first thrust the terrible plight of many children (and not only those in the dreadful slums) before the public gaze. The grim message of his books has been given greater publicity and impact in recent years through the medium of television. It will be recalled that the wide range of treatment for children's ailments available today did not exist in Dickens's time. The actual developments were slow, as the following chronology shows.

Liverpool's first Children's Hospital, the Royal Liverpool Children's Hospital, was established in Myrtle Street Liverpool in 1851. Today, we possess the largest children's hospital in Europe, at **Alder Hey Children's Hospital**, Eaton Road, West Derby, which was founded about 1910. A brochure supplied by Alder Hey (1995) contains some startling (and laudable) statistics:

¤ **84,000 attendances recorded in the A & E Department** alone in 1994.

¤ **78,000 images taken in the Radiology Dept. each year** (including X-rays, CAT-scans, gamma camera images, etc.).

¤   **198,000 tests each year in the Pathology Lab.**, to identify health problems, keep track of children's progress etc.

¤   **The longest continuous mural in the world** can be seen on the walls of its ground-floor corridor. It is incredibly long, startlingly exciting and extremely wide-ranging. It is currently being refurbished (1995). All of these are Firsts.

Many readers will be regular supporters of the Alder Hey Hospital Appeal and especially the annual Garden Fete. It has become one of Merseyside's "musts" on the social calendar,- but no Liverpudlian is under any illusion as to the real purpose behind the social aspect of the occasion.

1857: The first children's ward in any infirmary in Britain was opened in the Royal Southern Hospital (now no longer in existence). This same infirmary became **the first in the country to have an X-ray Dept.**, and was **the first to give artificial sunlight treatment**.

It was over 100 hundred years later, in 1959, that the first Mass **X-ray Campaign** ever was held in Liverpool. Nearly eighty per cent of the population over 15 years of age were X-rayed, and this led to the discovery of 2,776 significant cases of lung tuberculosis and 161 cases of lung cancer. Some 14,000 voluntary workers helped to run the month-long campaign. (D.P., 27th May 1969.)

1883: Cruelty to animals (see below) received much earlier attention than cruelty to children – and the reader may well have his or her own observations to make about the order of priority in that sequence of events. In fact, it was during an address by a local MP in Liverpool Town Hall to a meeting of the Society for the Prevention of Cruelty to Animals, that he happened to throw in a remark to the effect that it would also not be a bad idea to have a home for maltreated children. The result was the establishment of the **Liverpool Society for the Prevention of Cruelty to Children** (LSPCC).

The idea was late in arriving because of the attitude of the age towards children. They were largely regarded as "little adults" – adults waiting to grow up. Paintings and early photographs show them dressed in scaled-down versions of adult dress – the boys wearing jacket, waistcoat, long trousers, and large cap while the girls were smaller mirror images of mama. This persisted into this century, as did the nationally held tenet that "children should be seen and not heard". The writer can recall this dictum in operation in his childhood days.

Far worse, of course, was the maltreatment of children by adults generally. In the poorer areas of Liverpool, children were all too commonly working by the age of twelve – as chimney sweeps (see Dickens or Charles Kingsley), as extra help on barrows in the markets, as child minders, as scavengers or

The NSPCC building

trained thieves, and even as entertainers in pubs. Here they were often to be found singing or dancing on the pub tables until the early hours to entertain the drinkers sitting there in an alcoholic haze (a photograph in the Saddle Inn in Dale Street illustrates this). The ultimate degradation – child prostitution – was as prevalent then as it appears to be today.

We have to thank a Liverpool agent of the Bank of England, Mr T.F.A. Agnew, who had been to New York and had seen the work being done there to protect children, for the idea of forming the LSPCC in Islington Square. Fifteen months after the establishment of the Liverpool Society, a similar Society was started in London. The LSPCC was a First to be proud of, and the building where it all began is still standing, at the corner of Moss Street and New Islington (a bright-red brick building in Victorian style). It was later merged with the NSPCC, and, in 1954, became the National Society for the Prevention of Cruelty to Children (NSPCC).

Cruelty to Animals

Examples of cruelty to animals can be traced far back into history. The Step Pyramid of Sakkara, Egypt, was built to contain the dead carcasses of sacred cows which had died, or had been killed for ceremonial purposes. At their interment, their handlers were also killed and interred with the sacred animals (which seemed like a good case for the creation of a society for the prevention of cruelty to servants!).

More recent history demonstrates the brutality inflicted by men and women on domestic animals which were often cruelly used – cock-fighting, bear-baiting, dog-fighting, and rat-fighting were all regaled as acceptable pursuits in Georgian and Victorian times, for instance. Today, of course, the campaigns against hare coursing and fox-hunting are hotly pursued, but, again, the moral debate is not for these pages. It is not surprising to find that there were people who abhorred those activities where wanton cruelty was inflicted on animals, and decided to do something about it.

1809: The **first animal welfare organisation in the country was established in Liverpool**. It was called the **Society for the Suppression of Wanton Cruelty to Brute Animals**, and it met with immediate and violent opposition from vested interests: carters, the makers of whips, goads, muzzles, etc.; the organisers of hunts or Mains (a term in cock-fighting) and other deliberately cruel sports or commercial activities – (e.g. the use of pit ponies in mines).

This society survived and became the fore-runner of the RSPCA. The first RSPCA Branch in Liverpool was opened in 1841, though it was not the first branch in the country. Many of the early pioneers of the RSPCA were beaten up by thugs hired, allegedly, by carters.

General Medical Advances

Late **1700s:** John Lyon, who founded the Medical Library at the corner of Hope Street and Mount Pleasant, is credited with being "**the originator of approximating (bringing together) skin edges following amputation**, instead of the practice of constantly dressing an open wound". (*Liverpolitana*, P.H. Williams, 1971.)

Lowndes (1745-1831) was the Police Surgeon who **successfully campaigned against the practice of kissing the Bible** when an oath was being taken in court. (P.H. Williams, *op cit.*)

1776: Ether was first publicly used in Britain, as an anaesthetic, in Liverpool.

1804: John Bostock, a local doctor, discovered that **carbon dioxide is formed in the digestive process**. In 1806 he identified the **three primary constituents of bodily fluids** and he was **the first to give a complete description of Hay Fever** and its symptoms (1819).

1819: Another local doctor, James Carson, developed the artificial pneumothorax for pulmonary **tuberculosis** – i.e. the collapsing of the diseased lung.

1838: Dr Formby (Liverpool) **first used chloroform in liquid form.**

1840: Dr R. **Bickersteth** of Liverpool became the first physician to use the **carbolic spray and anti-septic catgut for completing surgical operations,** both minor and major. He was also the **first surgeon ever to adopt a special gown in which to operate,** instead of the traditional blood-stained top coat.

1846: A Liverpool chemist, David Waldie (1813-1889), first **discovered the potential of the liquid form of chloroform** when he used it at the old Myrtle Street Ear and Eye Hospital. He told Sir James Simpson about this – and the latter became the accredited discoverer of this potent anaesthetic. Perhaps this entry may help to set the record straight. In Bickerton's account, (Bickerton, *op cit,* page 137), Waldie describes how he and his colleagues, Dr Duncan and Dr Keith, tried it on themselves. On the first night, " we were all 'under the table' in a minute or two".

It also seems that Waldie had tried it with his friend John Abraham for we read, "Mrs Abraham, on one occasion, going back into the dining room at 87, Bold Street, was somewhat taken aback to find both men lying unconscious on the floor." Dedicated research indeed.

Yet it was not appreciated by everybody. One pious old clergyman "fervently denounced the use of chloroform in childbirth," declaring that Simpson and his colleagues were flouting God's ordinance, "In sorrow thou shalt bring forth children". This was woman's punishment for her "great original transgression" in the Garden of Eden. Another clergyman referred to chloroform as the "decoy of Satan". Simpson refuted these arguments by reminding them that the first surgical operation mentioned in the Bible was performed under an anaesthetic, for, at the creation of Eve, "..the Lord God caused a deep sleep to fall upon Adam, and he slept: and He took one of his ribs, and closed up the flesh instead thereof." *(Bickerton,* page 137)

1866: There still exists an age-old practice of pulling out a loose tooth by tying a piece of string to the offending tooth, then tying the other end of the string to the door-knob. A quick slam of the door jerks out the tooth! Painful as this may seem, it pales into total insignificance against an entry in the logbook of Christ Church School, Bootle. Several boys complained of tooth-ache. Whereupon, one of the masters extracted 9 teeth in less than five minutes! The "how" of the matter has never been revealed, but this rate of extraction must surely be a First!

1886: The First purpose-built **ambulance** was introduced in Liverpool in 1886 by Major William Joynson, Chairman of the Northern Hospital (once at the corner of Leeds Street near the Docks, but now demolished). He, too, brought the idea back from a visit to New York where horse-drawn ambulances had been introduced. (D.P: 21st April 1969.)

1886: A further claim for the **first ambulance** (though not purpose-built) can be made on behalf of Liverpool City Police.(See: Police.)

1889: Epilepsy has always been a most disturbing experience, both for the epileptic and for the person dealing with the epileptic. The first record of an epileptic colony was in Germany, and in 1889, **Britain's first epileptic colony** was established at **Maghull.** Today, Maghull Homes still accommodate some 130 people with epilepsy.

1896: The first **milk kitchen in the country** was set up in St Helens about 1896. The third Medical Officer for Health for St Helens, Dr Drew Harris, and some Councillors went on a fact-finding mission to a small town in Normandy where there was a milk kitchen. Sterilised (boiled) sweetened milk was fed to mothers unable to breast-feed for one penny (old penny) per day. They returned the empty bottles and collected a new lot each day. Two Lady Sanitary Inspectors supervised the preparation of the feeds, weighed babies and advised mothers. These were **the first Health Visitors and the first Infant Welfare Clinics.**

1898: Liverpool became the **first city to appoint a Municipal Bacteriologist,** Professor Rupert Boyce, Prof. of Pathology and Bacteriology at University College (Liverpool). He was appointed city analyst.

1900: Liverpool began the building, in Delamere Forest, of Britain's first **Public Sanatorium** for the open-air treatment of tuberculosis.

1901: First **anti-tubercular campaign in Britain**, in Liverpool.

1915: Liverpool had established Health Visitors before the 1915 national legislation, which "empowered" but did not "require" the formation of Health Clinics. (See **1920.**)

1920: Councils had to provide clinics, etc. Welfare centres were set up to supply milk for the artificial feeding of babies – the fore-runners of National Ante-natal and Post-natal Clinics.

1933: Among the list of advances in **anaesthesia**, mention must be made of the work of **Dr R.J. Minnett,** to whom a plaque was dedicated at his home in Kremlin Drive, Stoneycroft. Working at the Maternity Hospital, Dr Minnett was **the first in the world to provide greater freedom from pain in childbirth by administering a mixture of gas and air while the patient remained conscious.** It was called "Minnett Gas".

1944: T. Cecil Gray, from Crosby, was the **first doctor to use the drug curare** (a muscle relaxant) **in conjunction with an anaesthetic,** in 1944. He later became Professor of Anaesthesia at Liverpool University. Curare is more popularly known as the deadly poison used by South American Indians who tipped their arrow-heads with it for stunning their prey when hunting.

The "bonesetters of Crosshall Street" gained a reputation for their **unorthodox means of re-setting badly set broken limbs**. The first, Evan Thomas, lived in Crosshall Street and was considered a quack by many, but, though unqualified, he possessed a natural talent for resetting broken bones. Learning from his own experience of trying to work in a profession without the necessary qualifications, he determined to send his son to medical school to obtain them, and he worked hard to that end.

His qualified son, Hugh Owen Thomas (born in Liverpool in 1834, he practised at 11, Nelson Street), was the one who actually earned the sobriquet "bonesetter" because of his rather unusual bedside manner when treating his patients. The story is told (and is now legendary) that his surgery had curtains hanging all round the "operating table". Hugh Owen would position the limb to be reset on the table, then disappear behind the curtains for some moments. He would suddenly reappear, leaping through the curtains and wielding a mallet which he would bring down sharply on the wrongly-set bone, so re-breaking it and enabling it to be properly set. For the patient it must have given an entirely new meaning to the phrase, "a bone-shaking experience".

He was not accepted by the medical establishment, but he is known as the father of **orthopaedics. He published _Knee, Hip and Ankle_** at his own expense, but it was ignored in Britain. The American medical fraternity regarded it as a pioneering masterpiece. Hugh Owen also invented a special knee sling which proved invaluable in dealing with difficult knee wounds in the terrible trench warfare of WW1.

Hugh Owen's nephew, Sir Robert Jones, completed the trio who made Liverpool the cradle of orthopaedics as a branch of medicine. Sir Robert Jones is commemorated by a bas-relief in Liverpool Cathedral – just opposite the foundation stone. He is said to have produced the **first** ever British **X-rays** in Nelson Street in 1895 (unconfirmed First).

1966: Work at Liverpool University led to the discovery of the means of preventing Rhesus negative babies. (See also: Liverpool University.)

Wash-houses and Kitty Wilkinson

If ever anybody deserved a place in history for her concern for her fellow beings, the outstanding example must surely be Kitty Wilkinson. Her whole life, it might be said, made history. All the main elements were there: tragedy, drama, saintly perseverance, totally unselfish service to her neighbours, tremendous patience, indomitable determination, and an unfathomable

Kitty Wilkinson in the staircase window of the Anglican Cathedral

depth of true Christian charity. It was a life that was lived uncomplainingly from day to day, without worldly ambition, with unquenchable hope, and with a total commitment to alleviating the seemingly hopeless lot of the less fortunate. The inscription on her tombstone says it all: *"Indefatigable and self-denying, she was the widow's friend, the support of the orphan, the fearless and unwearied nurse of the sick, the instigator of Baths and Wash-houses for the poor."* The inscription ends with Mark 12, 44: *"They all did cast in of their abundance, but she of her want did cast in all that she had, even all her living."*

If a final accolade were needed, it exists (for posterity to observe and ponder upon) in the famous stained glass window in Liverpool Cathedral where are depicted "The Noble Women of the Staircase Window" (the title of the Rev William McNeill's little book on this subject), of whom Kitty is one.

Kitty was born Catherine Seaward in Londonderry, in 1786. When she was only a few years old, her working class parents took the Irish ferry to Liverpool in order to better themselves. At the mouth of the Mersey, their ship struck the Hoyle Bank, and her mother and sister were drowned. How she and her father managed for the next few years is hard to imagine. When she was ten, an old lady engaged her to run messages and to accompany her when she went to distribute food and clothing to the poor – Kitty's first experience of helping those less fortunate than herself.

The wash-house, Upper Frederick Street

At the age of twelve, she went to work in a cotton mill in Caton, near Lancaster, and, as an apprentice, had several privileges, not the least being the opportunity of improving her education at night school. She left the mill and went into service for a few years, then married a sailor, Sadly, soon afterwards, he was lost at sea, and she was left a widow with two very young children – one a hopeless weakling and the other a new-born babe. In addition, she had to look after her stepmother who was blind and insane, and, with almost ridiculous hospitality, she opened her door to anyone who wanted help. At one time, she had a mother and family lodged with her, and on another occasion, a blind invalid neighbour whom she looked after for seven years.

After the death of her stepmother, she came back to Liverpool where she was to learn that conditions were far worse than at Caton. "Poor people lived in cramped, crowded conditions in courts, alleys and cellars, with darkness, dirt and destitution for their constant companions." (Rev. McNeill, *op cit.*) She took in washing to be put through the mangle in her own wash-house to earn a little money. She took in three motherless children and, when their father died, brought them up as her own. She met and married a young man she had first met in Caton, Tom Wilkinson, who was a porter in Mr Rathbone's warehouse. They settled down in her house in Denison Street. Tom was also an hospitable man, so their home soon took on the status and atmosphere of an orphanage!

In 1832, cholera broke out in Liverpool (there were ten outbreaks between 1832 and 1840, according to one source). Kitty plunged in with her customary fervour and fearlessness. The only boiler in the street was in her scullery, so she offered the use of it to her neighbours to wash affected clothes and bed-linen. They accepted the offer so enthusiastically that she had to fit up her cellar as a wash-house, with the additional intention of using it as a disinfecting room for the clothes from the cholera homes and those which had not yet been infected by cholera. She managed it so well that not one of her workers became infected. **The idea of a public wash-house was born**.

(Terms like "infection" and "epidemic" probably did not exist at that time because it was thought that illness was brought by "bad air" ("miasma"). The term "plague" was more popularly used. The idea of germs being responsible was yet to materialise.)

When the cholera epidemic passed, there were many fatherless and motherless children who were neglected and even living rough. Kitty took in twenty of them every morning and read stories to them and taught them hymns in her bedroom. They enjoyed themselves so much that Kitty was forced to hire a room and employ another woman to teach them. Thus began the **South Corporation Infant School**, the **first public Infant School on Merseyside**. (First in the country?)

Her other acts of care and support are too numerous to be recorded here. Fuller accounts can be found in any public library. The city fathers rewarded her with the gift of a tea service and a silver teapot, and in 1846 she and Tom were made the first superintendents of the new **Public Baths – the first in Liverpool and in the country** - in Frederick Street. Tom died in 1848. Kitty outlived him by twelve years, to die at the age of 73.

Medical Officer of Health

Liverpool was **the first city anywhere to appoint a Medical Officer of Health,** on 1st January 1847, as a result of the **Liverpool Sanatory Act of 1846** (which predated a national act by several months). He was Dr Duncan who was, until recently, commemorated by a pub, The Dr Duncan, at the top of Seel Street on the left-hand side as one ascends towards Berry St. In fact, he was born in a house nearly opposite the pub, now known as The Blue Angel – of Beatles fame.

He was a physician to the Dispensaries and a lecturer in Jurisprudence in the School of Medicine, and he had been largely responsible for procuring the new Act. Shortly afterwards, the Commission on the Health of Towns published its report, and the public "..began to see that much of the misery, the moral degradation, the death, and the crime of the land, were preventable. " (Bickerton, *op cit*, p.175.)

His first report to the Council, in 1844, had been received with almost total disbelief. It showed that, based on the 1841 Census, "the population of Liverpool Parish amounted to 223,05, of whom about 160,000 may be estimated to belong to the working classes, and of these it is well known that a large proportion inhabits courts and cellars." (op cit, page 168)

The attempts to clear these cellars met with fierce opposition, and Duncan wrote in 1851 that: "To bring a cellar within the provision of the Act, the Magistrates require proof of its being occupied *during the night* and in order to withold this proof, parties are in the habit of removing or concealing in the daytime the beds or sacks, straws or shavings which they use as bedding." (*op cit* page 169)

In short, his report to the Health Committee revealed that we had the most unhealthy port in western Europe. The Council were eventually convinced of the accuracy and integrity of Dr Duncan's findings, and an immediate cleansing of infested houses was carried out. Walls were washed with lime (to eradicate bugs, cockroaches and the like) and offensive rubbish etc. removed.

Sadly, the Irish Potato Famine occurred about this time, and Liverpool was suddenly inundated with the arrival of some half-a-million immigrants in varying states of distress. Those who could afford it emigrated to the USA,

Canada, New Zealand and Australia, the rest had to be accommodated in Liverpool. The only accommodation available was in the cellars and slums that had just been cleansed. The whole sorry process began all over again.

Again, the reader is urged to read Bickerton (and others, in the Picton Library) for the full story of this awful time in our history and the magnificent work of men like Dr Duncan in overcoming prejudice, apathy and the rest of the official armoury of lethargy in order to get something done about it.

Dr Duncan: first Medical Officer of Health

The Workhouse – Agnes Jones

William Rathbone, perhaps the best-known of this great Liverpool family with its long tradition of service to our community, was appalled by the terrible conditions that existed in the Liverpool Workhouse on Brownlow Hill. **It had the regrettable title of "the biggest workhouse in Europe",** with a population of 5000. He highlighted especially conditions in the Workhouse Hospital, where "the incapable ministered to the incapable". He appealed in vain to the Guardians of the Workhouse to put an end to this terrible reproach to Liverpool, but who cared what went on in the workhouse? In the end, he offered to pay all the costs for three years if the Guardians would permit him to install a proper nursing system. This was agreed.

In 1864, he wrote to Agnes Jones to ask her to undertake the job of Superintendent of the Workhouse Hospital. The request came at a time when Agnes Jones, who had had her nursing career interrupted several times by family demands to nurse sick relations for long periods; finally became free of such responsibility. (As a practising Christian, for her, family came first.) She accepted and commenced her duties in the spring of 1865.

She found conditions absolutely appalling, so she tackled this Herculean task with typical common sense. She collected some 40 or 50 nurses, who were more or less competent, and hired a veritable army of ex-pauper women called "scourers" whose job was to scrub the building out, literally from top

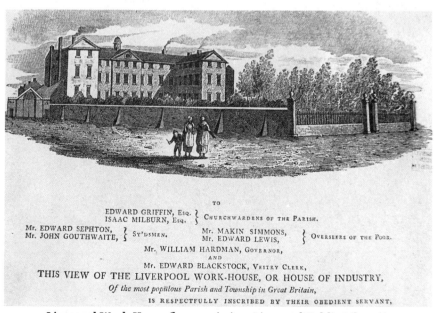

TO

EDWARD GRIFFIN, Esq. ⎱ Churchwardens of the Parish.
ISAAC MILBURN, Esq. ⎰

Mr. EDWARD SEPHTON, ⎱ Sy'dsmen.   Mr. MAKIN SIMMONS, ⎱ Overseers of the Poor.
Mr. JOHN GOUTHWAITE, ⎰   Mr. EDWARD LEWIS, ⎰

Mr. WILLIAM HARDMAN, Governor,

AND

Mr. EDWARD BLACKSTOCK, Vestry Clerk,

THIS VIEW OF THE LIVERPOOL WORK-HOUSE, OR HOUSE OF INDUSTRY,

Of the most populous Parish and Township in Great Britain,

IS RESPECTFULLY INSCRIBED BY THEIR OBEDIENT SERVANT,

Liverpool Work-House (by permission, Liverpool Public Library)

Agnes Jones, 1832-1868, in the staircase window of the Anglican Cathedral

to bottom. Years of neglect made this an appalling task with various spillages (human and otherwise) ingrained into the wooden floors. All the time that this exercise was being completed, there was the normal running of a hospital to be undertaken. Agnes Jones herself worked from five in the morning till eleven at night.

She continued her heroic and exhausting work until she became infected with typhus (most likely from a workhouse inmate) and died in February 1868 – less than three years after taking up her post. She too is commemorated in the "Staircase Window of Noble Women" in Liverpool Cathedral. She was taken back to her native Ireland to be buried at Fahan. Her passing was mourned by many, not least by Florence Nightingale herself.

District Nursing Service

Meanwhile, Rathbone had written to invite Florence Nightingale to come to Liverpool to train local women for nursing the poor in their homes. This idea

arose from his high regard for the wonderful nursing care given to his wife, when she had been very ill, by Nurse Mary Robinson. Florence Nightingale's reply indicated that she thought the best way forward lay in recruiting local women for training by local nurses – though she would, of course, advise where and when she could. Rathbone's guiding light was the admiration he had for Mary Robinson's selfless devotion to duty and her absolute professionalism (she had been trained by Florence Nightingale many years before). **The first District Nursing Service was born** in 1855 at Solio Street.

Florence Nightingale's assistance in establishing the District Nursing Service

The Florence Nightingale memorial at the corner of Upper Parliament Street and Princes Road

is commemorated by a fine relief in stone at the corner of Princes Road and Upper Parliament Street.

School of Tropical Medicine

At the Pier Head, close to the ferry building, stands a fine stone plinth supporting three bronze figures. At the top is a female figure, representing Liverpool, holding a liner in her hand. To the left of the plinth (as one faces inland), is a seated female figure with many tropical fruits in her lap, including bananas, and to the right, another seated female figure holding a microscope. Below the top figure is a plaque dedicated to Sir Alfred Lewis Jones (1845-1909), to whose memory the monument was erected in 1913 (Sculptor: Sir George Frampton)

The left-hand female figure recalls Sir Alfred's early life as a young man on the administrative staff of Elder Dempster Line, whose steamships were familiarly known in Liverpool as the "banana boats". It was Sir Alfred who **promoted the eating of bananas in Britain, where they had never been seen before.** A local newspaper remarked that the high cost of bananas seemed to suggest that "bananas were for the classes, not the masses."

The right-hand figure commemorates the establishment of the **first School of Tropical Medicine** in the world by Sir Alfred, in Liverpool, in 1898. It was somewhat late in arriving because the dreadful sufferings associated with tropical diseases had been experienced by sailors and travellers for a long time. The School's first big success was the discovery, by Sir Ronald Ross, that **malaria was transmitted by the bite of the anophiles mosquito.** For this brilliant breakthrough, Ross was awarded the **Nobel Peace Prize in 1902.** Other discoveries connected with the School include:

¤ **1900:** The parasite that causes **elephantiasis.**

¤ **1901:** The origins of **sleeping sickness.**

¤ **1905:** The cause of **tick fever.**

The School – which is a charity – continues its fight against disease within a formidable list of fields of research: child health in developing countries, parasitology, entomology, tropical paediatrics, epidemiology, molecular biology and immunology, endemic and infectious diseases, and, of course, malaria. Researchers are available for talks to societies and groups, and the writer can personally recommend the absorbing interest of these slide talks – though a strong stomach may be required for one or two of the more hideous examples of tropical diseases!

The School employs some 185 academics, research and support staff. Students numbered 345 from 67 countries, according to the Annual Report for 1995/96. Courses range from 3-year PhD research programmes to one-week summer courses.

The Alfred Jones memorial, Pier Head, in front of the MD&HB building

Hospitals

Hospitals have earned their places on the Roll of Honour of Firsts. Alder Hey has already been mentioned as have others, but the list is far from complete.

1896: The **first X-ray machine in Great Britain** was installed at the Southern Hospital (now demolished), and the **first medical diagnosis by X-ray** was carried out there. The **first special children's ward** was opened there in **1857** (already cited), as well as one of the first pathological laboratories.

Not only was the Royal Liverpool Children's Hospital **the oldest provincial hospital for children** (founded by Stephens with funds largely provided by Matthew Gregson, a local historian), but it also established a tradition of long-term stays at a special branch of the hospital at Heswall, on the Dee coast of the Wirral. (The climate of that area helped. It is said to have 200 hours more sunshine per year than the national average.) Regrettably, the Heswall Hospital was closed down a few years ago.

Stanley Hospital, Bootle, was one of the **first general hospitals**. It also **claimed to be the first to allow a woman doctor on its staff**. For a short time Walton Hospital (which began life as a workhouse founded by West Derby Union, and claimed 3,000 births out of 600,000 births in Britain) was **the most comprehensive hospital in Europe**. It later (post-World War 2) gained a wide reputation for its Neuro-Surgery Unit.

1971: Mill Road Hospital claimed to be the **largest maternity hospital in England**.

Liverpool City Council's Contribution

Credit must be given to past City Councils for their backing for many local advances in health care (the first in the country to do so). Their contribution included the appointment of the first Medical Officer of Health, the employment of women Health Visitors to visit slums and to give advice on general health matters, the appointment of Britain's first Borough Engineer in 1840, and the promotion of several private and radical Acts of Parliament, ahead of national legislation, in the 1830s and 1840s. The latter included: the appointment of the first ever Municipal Building Inspectors, a Health Committee, a Libraries' Committee, free public libraries, the first public washhouse (in the world) in 1842, and the first day nursery. They also claimed brand new powers – to control the width of streets, to dispose of sewage, to take over water supply from private enterprise bodies (which were boosting water prices by artificially created shortages) and to plan a reservoir.

PARKS & GARDENS

When all has been said about those hectic and exciting forms of exercise we practised when we were younger, those of us who have "reached the sere and yellow leaf" prefer something a little gentler! A stroll in one of the Merseyside Parks is welcome, or in the North Wales hill country. Merseyside led the way in providing parks – referred to as "the lungs of the city" last century.

1847: Birkenhead Park opened. It was designed by Sir Joseph Paxton, famous for his Chatsworth House and his Crystal Palace designs. He was assisted by Hornblower. Its landscaped walks, Swiss Bridge, lake, and cricket grounds, were the main components of the first Public Park in the world – that is, **the first Park to be created with public funds**. It was very highly regarded, and attracted an American, Ormstead, from New York who was most impressed. So much so, that on his return he set about the creation of New York Central Park, based on Paxton's ideas.

Prince's Park: This park, at the end of a French style boulevard, was the work of Monsieur André of Paris with the English gardener, Hornblower. The Boulevard and park were completed and given to the public for its use by Yates. **It was the first privately sponsored park to be given to the public.**

Sefton and **Stanley Parks:** Named after the two local Earls, these parks were completed in the mid-19th century, at the south and north ends of the city respectively. The more beautiful of the two was Sefton Park with its large, arc-shaped lake (formed by damming an existing stream called the Jordan), small waterfall, Palm House, statue of Eros (a copy of the one in Piccadilly Circus) and the pirate boat *Jolly Roger*. Sadly, vandalism has marred the statue, the boat and the Palm House, but a determined effort is now under way to restore these features. A most beautiful addition has been the Daffodil Fields where, initially, one million bulbs were planted in 1991 by the Marie Curie Foundation for Cancer Research. It is a most moving site to see when all the daffodils are blooming, and it is all in a very good cause.

Stanley Park has been diminished by neglect and vandalism. The glass pavilion, from which people used to view, through their telescopes, the ships coming and going in the Mersey and Liverpool Bay, has been rebuilt, but further vandalism has occurred. At the opposite end of the Park, a large car park serves the two local teams, Everton and Liverpool, on alternate Saturdays, but it does nothing to enhance the Park (which also has a small lake).

Calderstones Park: This is a name shrouded in mystery. What were the stones? The most likely answer seems to be, that they were a burial place (a passage grave) for a prominent leader or chieftain of the Boat People who lived in their ships off the west coast of Europe – somewhat in the manner of the Vikings much later on. They rarely came ashore, except to trade or bury prominent leaders. The Park is beautifully laid out, with several attractive features, including a Japanese Garden. It used to have large glasshouses containing possibly the finest collection of orchids in the UK, if not further afield. Unfortunately, the wilder elements in the Militant brotherhood forced the destruction of the glasshouses, to their everlasting shame.

Parks also exist, smaller and larger, round the City (Newsham, Stanley Park, Bootle, Camp Hill Woolton, Allerton, and Blackwood – the oldest in the area.)

International Garden Festival

Once again, the good wine has been kept until last. The Liverpool IGF (May to October 1984) was opened by Her Majesty on May 8th, and was a wonderful success. It contained a host of innovative work, based on filling the famous Cast Iron Shore with 30 million tons of city rubbish, capped with clay and soil, then planted quite profusely with trees. The critics said it was a waste of plants and trees because the climate would kill them off. Today, (1997) the IGF site is possibly more beautiful than ever, if reduced in size. So much for the local wiseacres!

In England it was a First on the grand scale. Walks and "natural" sculptures; glorious gardens with international themes and foliage; and a beautiful Festival Hall with exhibitions from all over the world changing every fortnight. There was a miniature steam railway running round the site, with trains on loan from Southport and the Brighton and Hove Railway, carrying people round the huge site; the "Yellow Submarine" of Beatles fame, built by the apprentices at Cammell Lairds; and the Japanese and Chinese Gardens, separated by a small, man-made lake. Two vital benefits emerged from the IGF – it gave Liverpool back its pride, and raised a hope that has never been dimmed. It was **the start of an on-going fight-back. (Perhaps our most valuable First.)**

PEOPLE OF LIVERPOOL

A great number of prominent people in and around Liverpool made important contributions to the culture and life of the city, and many of them qualify for a First. Some are mentioned elsewhere (Kitty Wilkinson, Dr Duncan, Jesse Hartley, etc.) A few made contributions that we may not care to think too much about. As one well-known Liverpool entertainer has so often stressed on television, "That's Life!"

The Childe of Hale 1578-1623

In 1578, in the village of Hale (near Liverpool Airport), John Midleton was born. He was destined for a very special kind of fame and a First – namely, to be the **tallest man in the world** at that time. He grew to a prodigious 9ft 3ins It is said that his thigh bone was some 2ft 9ins long, while his hand was 18ins from middle-finger-tip to the base of his hand. The ceiling in the village cottage where he lived had to be taken up to the roof ridges to accommodate his height, and the hook on which he hung his coat was 10ft from the floor.

Sir Gilbert Ireland, Lord of the Manor of Hale and builder of Hale Hall in 1604, took John away from farm labouring to work as his personal bodyguard – to walk with him, to stand behind his chair at meals, and to perform feats of strength for his friends. King James I heard of this prodigy with his enormous height and strength and sent for him. Sir Gilbert took John to be presented to the King in London. The latter called for a match between John and the King's Champion who, though not as tall as John, was a wrestler of prodigious proportions and was more than his match. However, the latter won the day by snapping the Champion's thumb, then throwing him. John won the 20-guinea gold prize, but was robbed of it before he had reached Oxford on his way home. There is said to be a handprint of the Childe worked into a stone pier in Brasenose College, Oxford, and there is also a painting there of him.

Charwomen

1596: The earliest recorded instance in the country of the word "charwoman", occurs in the records of the Common Council, in 1596, wherein it was ordered that, " all yonge women, and others called charr women, in this towne, as are in noe service, shall place theim selves in some good and honest service."

The Man who Slept in his own Coffin

In St Nicholas's graveyard lies the body of a man who was prepared for death for over 25years. He was Captain Broadneaux, who served on the Royalist side in the first part of the Civil War, then on the Parliamentarian side in the second part of that dreadful conflict. At the age of 83 he became very ill and thought he was dying, so he ordered his coffin. An almost miraculous recovery followed, so he decided to be ready for death by **sleeping every night in his coffin! He died 26 years later!**

Sarah Biffin – Artist Without Arms, 1784-1850

Sarah Biffin ended her days at 8, Duke Street (now part of a commercial building). She was only one metre (39 ins) tall for she had been born without arms and legs (there has been some dispute about the latter disability, but her birth certificate resolves the argument.) Very early on, she was taken into a travelling circus as a freak in a side-show, with an agreement that she remain with the circus for 15 years and be taught to paint by the circus manager. She learned to paint by fixing the shaft of the brush to a metal loop on her right shoulder, then manipulating the brush with her mouth.

She was a quick learner, and could paint better than her teacher, the circus manager, within five years. He offered to let her leave the circus, but she insisted on keeping to her fifteen-year contract. Before her death, in Liverpool, she had been under the patronage of four crowned heads – George III, George IV, William IV and Queen Victoria – and her work was hung in the **Royal Academy.** Her final days were spent in unaccustomed comfort, thanks to the help she received from the Rathbones and other Liverpool families who befriended her.

First US Consul in the World

1790: The first United States Consul ever to be appointed anywhere in the world was **James Laury,** who was appointed to Liverpool by George Washington, from 1790 to 1819. He resided at 4, Rodney Street. He had been a classmate of **Thomas Jefferson**, another US President. Maury's son, Lieutenant Maury, US Navy, was born in Liverpool. James Maury's office was in Paradise Street, which was sited on the line of the old "pul", filled in when the first Wet Dock was constructed. (See: Thomas Steers.)

Felicia Dorothea Hemans, née Browne 1792-1835

Her birthplace was 118, Duke St. She wrote her first book of verse between the ages of 8 and 13, and continued to make her living as a poetess. She is probably best remembered for the opening line of her famous poem *Casabianca: "The boy stood on the burning deck...."*

She is remembered (and revered) by the Americans for her poem, *The Landing of the Pilgrim Fathers*, which is traditionally recited in America at each family circle at Thanksgiving. She was described by William Wordsworth, on her death, as "That Holy Spirit Sweet as the Spring, as Ocean deep."

She also lived for a time in Picton Road, Wavertree. The site of her house is now occupied by a garage (the first garage past the traffic lights, coming from Liverpool city centre).

First English Girls' High School

The first English Girls' High School was opened in Blackburne House, Hope Street, in 1844. The House was a gift to the city from a former Mayor, John Blackburne, who had built it as his country house. The same building has since been converted to a **Centre of Excellence for Women**, to improve their chances of gaining higher positions in commerce, industry, etc., in this man's world. (First in Lancashire?)

William Ewart Gladstone

W.E. Gladstone (1809-1898) is renowned for the fact that he was **Prime Minister of the UK for four Parliaments**: 1868-74, 1880-1885, 1886, and 1892-1894. He was born and bred at 62, Rodney Street, Liverpool, and became the greatest Liberal statesman in our history. Though not particularly popular with Queen Victoria, who found him boring, he was responsible for some of the greatest reforms and attempted to get Home Rule for Ireland. His name was used for the Gladstone Bag – "a light, leather portmanteau, hinged so as to open flat into two approximately equal compartments." (The Oxford Illustrated Dictionary) The reader will be aware of the many books written about this great man.

Prime Minister Assassinated by Liverpool Man

1812: John Bellingham (1771-1812) was a native of St Neots who came to Liverpool in the early 19th century and resided in one of the terraced houses in Duke Street, He was the only man ever to assassinate a Prime Minister. Bellingham was a timber contractor who went to Russia to further his business, but while there, he was arrested and imprisoned for debt. He applied to the British Ambassador for assistance, but this was refused. Eventually he was released and returned to Britain and Duke Street.

He brooded on the fact that he had been let down badly by the British Government and sought redress for the injustice he claimed he had suffered at the hands of the Russians. His appeal failed, and this perceived neglect and insult rankled. In May 1812, he purchased two pistols in London, managed to enter the Houses of Parliament, then shot dead Prime Minister Spencer Perceval in the Lobby of the House of Commons. In less than a week, Bellingham was arrested, tried, convicted, sentenced and executed. One kills a Prime Minister at one's extreme peril.

President Lincoln Assassinated by Liverpool Man

1865: An unwanted First. Julius Brutus Booth was a popular actor who often played at the old Theatre Royal (1772-1884) in Williamson Square (the theatre later became the Cold Storage Co., building). Booth and his family emigrated to America in 1821. His younger son, John Wilkes Booth, assassinated **Abraham Lincoln in Ford's Theatre, Washington, in 1865 – the first man to assassinate an American President.** The predominance of the world of the theatre in this tragic tale is a strange coincidence. Coincidence may be even more apparent in the fact that the Theatre Royal was sited in a Williamson Square which had badly degenerated from the pleasing ethos of its foundation (mid -18th century) to being the hub of the town's vice and crime by the end of the 18th century. Had the young John Wilkes Booth absorbed something of its evil atmosphere, perhaps, to lead him on to his dreadful crime? An interesting speculation.

Two who Cheated the Hangman

Two of the most sensational trials in English legal history took place in Court Number 1 in St George's Hall. The earlier trial was of Florence Maybrick in 1899 for allegedly murdering her husband by the frequent administration of arsenic, derived from flypapers, via his food. Amidst conflicting evidence and high drama, the Jury were misdirected by the Judge, and returned a verdict of "Guilty." The Judge donned the black cap, and the execution date was fixed. At that point, public opinion in Liverpool erupted into heated demands for the release of Mrs Maybrick, on the grounds of an unfair trial. Prayers were offered in the city and a petition sent to the House of Lords. **For the first time in legal history, the death sentence was commuted – to 15 years in gaol in the South of England.** She outlived all her accusers, and even returned to Aintree for the Grand National in 1927. She died in poverty back in her native Virginia after WW2.

The second instance was the Wallace Case. Herbert William Wallace worked for the Prudential Insurance Co., in Liverpool. He allegedly murdered his wife by beating her brains in, then established an alibi for himself, based on his visiting a street that did not exist, in the Liverpool suburb of Woolton. The Defence cleverly presented their case on the grounds that the whole case hinged on the time factor. Could Wallace have gone (by tram) to Menlove Gardens East (which did not exist) and back, within the times he was seen? Again, public opinion switched completely round, in Wallace's favour, when the Judge appeared to misguide the Jury, resulting in the death sentence being passed. Prayers were said at Liverpool Cathedral, and a Petition sent to the House of Lords. **For the first time in legal history, the Death Sentence was quashed,** and Wallace walked free. He died of cancer at Clatterbridge Hospital two years later.

Both cases still cause controversy. They also ensure full coachloads of thrill-seeking passengers on the popular Murders and Mysteries tours of Liverpool, conducted by MerseyGuides, and held during the dark nights when the scenes of the crimes are visited. Again, the reader is recommended to participate.

St James's Cemetery, Hope Street

It may seem most unusual, if not downright macabre, to claim Firsts for a cemetery, but St James's Cemetery can justify such claims. It is sited in a quarry once used to supply stone for many of our major buildings (e.g. the Town Hall). Its particular claim to fame arose from the chalybeate spring which still emerges from the foot of the east wall. This spring had healing properties, especially for certain eye troubles, and was used by local doctors. It nearly led to Liverpool being declared a spa! Several interesting people are buried there whose contributions to the life and culture of Liverpool were unique in some way.

Sarah Biffin: (See above) Her gravestone can be located nearly opposite the spring that flows out of the east wall of the cemetery.

Captain John Oliver: His gravestone can be found among the gravestones, at the north end of the cemetery, which mark the resting places of many sea captains. His record of naval service was distinguished by the fact that **he fought in every sea battle in the Napoleonic Campaign and lived to tell the tale.** He died at home at the ripe old age of 104 years. (Assumed to be a First.)

William Huskisson: MP and former President of the Board of Trade, rests within the domed mausoleum near the spring in the east wall of St James's Cemetery (just below Liverpool Cathedral). He was killed on the opening day of the Liverpool – Manchester Railway, 15th September 1830, when he was run over by the *Rocket*. Huskisson had crossed the lines to speak to the Duke of Wellington when the *Rocket* was seen approaching. Some people saw his danger and shouted to warn him. He seemed to become confused, slipped, and fell, just as the *Rocket* was upon him. He was severely injured, one leg being badly crushed by the heavy driving wheels and the other one was completely severed. He died of his injuries that evening at a friend's house. He was the **first person in the world to be killed by a steam passenger engine.**

Baby Louise Bencke

John Albert Bencke was a highly regarded citizen of Liverpool. Born in Danzig on 8th November 1814, he came to Liverpool in 1835 and joined a firm prominent in the Russian trade. He was hard working, most efficient, and a great traveller. He was made Consul for Wurtemburg in 1858, and later received the title for life as Honorary Consul. He married Elizabeth Hughes (of London) and they had two children, Albert Henry (8th December 1846) and Louise Elizabeth (8th April 1851).

J.A. Bencke is buried in St John's Cemetery, Knotty Ash. Some years ago, his diary came into the writer's hands and was largely quoted in the writer's first book, *A History of West Derby* (co-author: David Power). The diary, written with hindsight, listed Bencke's travels all over Europe – too full to include here – which occurred with regular frequency. On one occasion, when "Baby" Louise was unwell, he decided on another "Continental trip and change of air for the sake of baby". This seemed an acceptable reason for leaving the smoke-polluted and damp atmosphere of Merseyside in those times.

Sadly, the journey was a gruelling one – via Hamburg, Schwerin, Rostock, Berlin, and Stettin to Danzig. It was here that baby Louise "died, sometime in August 1842 " (his diary entry for a most tragic family event). The next sentence in the diary reads, "..she was put in spirits of wine to be sent back to Liverpool where she was buried in St James's Cemetery, Croxteth Park".

The family then continued their tour, via Leipzig, Wiesenfeld, Eisenach and Frankfurt, where news reached him of his sister's death, but the tour continued, via Mayence, Bonn, Cologne, Brussels, Waterloo, and back to England. As an example of seemingly callous indifference the above takes some beating. He did not even have his daughter's burial place right – there is no St James's Cemetery, Croxteth Park. He possibly meant St James's by the Cathedral (above). Nor, apparently, was he concerned enough to get the date of her demise correct. On the other hand, he was writing in retrospect, so perhaps his earlier true feelings were deliberately suppressed.

(The writer has made one or two attempts to find the grave, but with no success to date.)

Jessie Crosbie

The late Liverpool writer, Frank Shaw, collected into one volume a delightful cross-section of Liverpool life, manners, customs, humour and people. It is called *My Liverpool* and has recently been reprinted. Probably the greatest character he met and described was Miss Jessie Crosbie, Headmistress of St Augustine's C of E School, Vauxhall. To tell too much of the story here would be to spoil an entertaining, courageous yet sad tale – with a sting in the tail.

All that need be said is that, because of the lean and hard times of the mid-twenties, Miss Crosbie started:

¤ the first **School Meals Service** by contacting local shops (Catholic and Protestant!) and "scrounging" food each day, which she cleaned and cooked with the help of one or two mothers, and served to the near-starving children at the school. She even paid for some out of her own pocket – and teachers' pay was abysmal in those days. ("Children can't learn if their bellies are empty.")

¤ the first **Evening Play Centre** so that her children, and children from the nearby St Francis Xavier's RC School (who had benediction every evening after school) could leave school at the same time, to be escorted to their homes by brothers, or fathers, or uncles or even the bigger truants from either school! After their evening meal, these same men were encouraged to patrol the ill-lit and dangerous streets and return children to their homes if they were found wandering. ("Children can't learn if they are falling asleep at their desks.")

¤ **school washrooms and baths** where begrimed children could be brought by their parents to be given a good scrub. Their mothers were exhorted to take the chance of bathing themselves. ("Children can't learn if they are irritated by dirt and nits.") The washing facilities were provided by a reluctant Education Office which simply caved in when faced by a very doughty and determined small woman who knew what she wanted – for her children – and would brook no opposition.

Nobody knew, until late in her life, that she had been awarded an MBE. It is a heart-warming story incorporating the evils of poverty, self-help in dire conditions, genuine love of children, real charity and the deep admiration of former pupils for a headmistress who never spared herself on their behalf.

Charley's Aunt

Brandon Thomas (1856-1914) was born at 101, Mount Pleasant. He became a shipyard worker, then journalist, author, and finally dramatist here in Liverpool. **He wrote the famous stage play** *Charley's Aunt* **which was still a theatre favourite in the author's early lifetime.**

First Woman Public Analyst

1956: It is claimed that Liverpool appointed Mrs Roberts as the first woman Public Analyst in the country.

First Woman Barrister

The first women barristers in the UK were Miss Fay Kyle and Miss A.K.S. Deverall who were called to the Irish Bar on 1st November 1921.

The first woman KC was Mrs Margaret Kidd of Scotland, followed by Miss Helena Normanton and Miss Rose Heilbron who became QCs on 12th April 1969. **Miss Heilbron, while engaged for a murder trial at Stafford Assizes, was appointed the first woman Recorder.** She succeeded Neville Laskie as Recorder of Burnley.

Oldest Chinese Community

It is claimed that Liverpool's Chinatown is the oldest established in Europe. This is not surprising if one considers the great number of Chinese who formed part of ships' crews during Liverpool's heyday as the biggest port of the Empire. Their New Year's celebrations are a well-established social event in the local calendar, and our Chinese restaurants play an equally prominent part in the local gourmets' dining-out programme.

Boy Scouts

1908: The first Scout troop in the world was formed in Birkenhead, following a visit by Lord Baden Powell. He expressed the view that street-corner gang leaders had most of the qualifications of leadership needed for Patrol Leaders, especially in activities like tracking and camping. The movement that began in Birkenhead spread throughout the world with more than 10 million Scouts being enrolled -including Harold Wilson and Paul McCartney.

Birkenhead later staged the first **Boy Scouts International Jamboree** at Arrowe Park in 1929. Taking part was a young Prince of Wales (later, the

Duke of Windsor), and the one thing everybody recalls of that great event was that it poured rain for the whole fortnight!

The Athenaeum

Liverpool's Athenaeum was **the first such organisation to be founded**, in 1797. This preceded Boston's (1807) by ten years, and London's (1824) by 27 years.

Ye Ugly Face Club

Also known as the Ugly Mug Club, the club was formed in Liverpool on 15th January 1743 with the grander title of *Ye Most Honorable and Facetious Society of Ugly Faces*. It remained in existence for eleven years, disbanding on 21st January 1754. Among its 55 members was said to be the architect of Liverpool Town Hall (John Wood the Elder of Bath).

The qualification for membership (drawn chiefly from the merchant class) was, that the aspiring candidate should exhibit **"something odd, remarkable, Drol or out of the way in his Phiz, as in the length, breadth, narrowness, or in his complexion, the cast of his eyes, or make of his mouth, lips chin, & co."**

So, the fortunate possessor of a deathbed complexion, a hedgehog forehead, squinting and/or pig eyes, a "monstrous long nose resembling a speaking trumpet", or one rising in the middle like a camel's hump, a fluke mouth with "irregular bad set of teeth like those of a worn-out comb thoroughly begrimed" and many, many more were assured of sympathetic consideration for membership! An excellent description of further "beauty spots" like the above, exhibited by the club members, can be found in *Liverpol Roundabout* by Richard Whittington-Egan. It makes hilarious reading. The Club must be considered a First because it is impossible to imagine anyone else in the world wanting to challenge for the honour of joining such a motley crew!

The World's First Air Hi-Jack

This entry is such an amazing story that the writer has cheated, just a little, by widening the sphere of Firsts to include Maghull and the Mediterranean! During WW2, Pilot Oficer Dunsmore, of Maghull, was the Navigator of a *Beaufort* Torpedo Bomber of 217 Squadron operating from Malta, searching for enemy shipping near Greece. A merchant ship was sighted and the attack was started. Torpedo bombing was a very special skill, but it was also highly dangerous because the plane had to head towards its target at a constant speed, at low level, and on a dead straight course. This was to ensure that the torpedo went into the sea at a pre-set depth and angle for accuracy. Obviously, a torpedo bomber was extremely vulnerable to anti-aircraft fire in these conditions, as Dunsmore's plane and crew discovered – to their cost. They were hit in one engine, then came the command to ditch.

The ditching was safely accomplished. They were picked up by an Italian *Cant* float seaplane and flown to the nearby island of Levkas. All four of the crew – Captain Edward Strever (Pilot), P/O William Martin Dunsmore (Navigator) and two New Zealand Sergeants, Alex Raymond Brown and John Wilkinson – were taken as prisoners of war, yet were wined and dined by the Italian Air Force Officers at the Levkas base.

The next day, they were put aboard another Italian *Cant* seaplane under armed guard, and told they would be flown to a proper POW camp at Taranto in Sicily. They decided that this wasn't a good idea at all, and further decided that they would exercise their right and duty to effect an escape. The *Cant* crew – normally a crew of four – had been augmented by an extra man to act as armed guard. He little realised he had become the centre of their undivided attention as they waited for a suitable chance to present itself. Eventually, Dunsmore persuaded the guard to look at something out of the plane's side window – and his job as an armed guard ended rather abruptly.

The RAF crew disarmed the Italians and tied them up. Then they examined their immediate problems: they had no idea where they were, they could not speak Italian, they had no air maps with which to navigate to Malta, and they had no idea of the fuel state. Bill Dunsmore made some rough sketch maps to try and show the Italians what he wanted to know, and a course was eventually set. The Italian Flight Engineer suddenly grew agitated and started calling, "Benzina. Benzina". They realised he was trying to tell them that fuel was running low, so they released his bonds and allowed him to switch over to the reserve tanks.

They eventually reached Malta – to be met by *Spitfires* coming up to challenge them. Pilot Edward Strever waggled the aircraft's wings, and Dunsmore took off his white shirt and waved it out of the window, hoping to convince the Spitfires that the *Cant's* intentions were not hostile. They landed in Maltese waters, just by St Paul's Bay – to be met by a boatload of armed sailors! The latter were dumbfounded to see an RAF crew climbing out of an Italian aircraft.

William (Bill) Dunmore and Edward Strever were each awarded a DFC, while John Wilkinson and Alexander Raymond Brown each received a DFM. Thus ended **the world's first air hijack!**

After the war, Bill Dunsmore became a well-known personality in Maghull, both as a shopkeeper (Dunsmore Hardware Stores) and eventually as a Squadron Leader in the ATC, Maghull Squadron.

(The writer wishes to thank Mrs Gillian Shipton, Bill Dunsmore's daughter, who telephoned the story from Hereford, where she is now living, and who is clearly very proud of her father!)

(Readers may recognise this story of heroism. It appeared in *Reader's Digest*, on Radio Merseyside some years ago, in Roy Nesbitt's *Torpedo Airman*, in Ralph Barker's *Down in the Drink*, and in an earlier BBC programme, *Focus*, presented by Vera McKechnie. Good stories, like good wine, deserve to be tasted often.)

After Sunday morning breakfast, or even before one's afternoon snooze, how about doing a crossword? **Crossword puzzles** – derived from a puzzle called a "Word-cross" – were devised by **Arthur Wynne, a Liverpool emigrant,** and first appeared in the "New York Sunday World" on 21st December 1913. It achieved instant popularity and became a regular feature. The rules were drawn up from readers' suggestions and were refined to popular taste. The diagonally symmetrical grid, now so familiar, was soon adopted, partly because it was pleasing to look at and partly because it was easier to proof-read. It is said that it was based on his grandfather's efforts to amuse him with "Double Acrostics" or "Magic Squares". By separating the words with blank spaces and adding a list of 32 clues, Wynne created the Crossword.

PUBLIC SERVICES

THE POLICE

The Liverpool City Police are proud of their Firsts, as the following items show. The local Force was set up in 1836 with 390 men initially. Most of these had previously been involved in the local watch brigades before joining up. (Note: Cheshire Police, 1829, was the first to be established outside London; Lancashire Constabulary was established in 1839.) The first Head Constable (equivalent to our Chief Constable today) was Michael Whitty, an Irishman from Rosslare, who started life as a reporter. Perhaps he deserves a First for the fact that, when he left the Police, he went back to his earlier profession of journalism and **set up his very own newspaper, the Daily Post**. (Quoted, appropriately, from the Daily Post for 17th April 1996!)

According to one claim, **Liverpool Police were the first Police Force to use helmets, and the first to be armed with cutlasses** (1836 to 1886). Such weapons would have been in plentiful supply after the Napoleonic and other wars, and Watch Committees, working on an economic shoestring, would have been glad to purchase cutlasses at war surplus prices.

The Watch Committee had a **horse ambulance by 1884**, stationed at the Northern Hospital (now demolished). Later, there was an ambulance stationed at the Royal Southern Hospital (demolished), the old Royal Infirmary (behind the University buildings) and Stanley Hospital, Bootle. **The Liverpool City Police replaced their wheeled litters (stretchers) with an ambulance which was modelled on those in use in the United States.**

Until WW2, the Fire Department was part of the Police Force – "H" Division, in fact, whose Officers adopted Naval Ranks. **In 1901 the first motorised Police Fire Engine was introduced** – the first of its type in Britain. A picture taken at the time (see book below) shows the first Fire Brigade group with the Deputy Superintendent of the Brigade (Chief Inspector Thomas). The machine was a Daimler motor chemical vehicle fitted with a body built at the Royal Coach Works in Hope Street. (Fellow MerseyGuide, John Edwards, thinks that it was probably the building next door to the Philharmonic Dining Rooms because there are signs of a garage type building there.) The picture also shows the machine fitted with an **alarm gong, first used in Liverpool in 1898**, to replace the former, less effective, whistle warning.

Liverpool Police were **the first to be equipped with rubber-sole boots** for night duty **(1889)**. They were warm – and quiet. London followed some months later.

1908: The Liverpool Police Tug-of-War team won a **Silver in the Olympic Games.**

1919: The first ever strike by the Police took place.

1925: The first **Juvenile Court in the land** was opened at 3A Crosshall Street in an old church building which can still be seen.

1948-9: Liverpool Police were **the first in the country to introduce a Juvenile Liaison Scheme** to help educate youngsters to appreciate their place in, and responsibility to, the community, and thus keep them out of further trouble.

1934: Liverpool Police were the first to have **two-way radio communication.** (Morse code messages at first – every mobile officer had to learn the Morse Code – and oral messages later.) The radio sets were kept in a leather satchel slung from the cross-bar of the policeman's bike. **Later, they were used in cars and on the beat.** The main transmitter, at Old Swan, was powerful enough to speak to a French station and to a trawler at sea off Bergen. It had one limitation – it had only one-way communication with motor-cycle combinations because the proper radio equipment for these machines was much too heavy. (D.P., 9th April 1969.)

Liverpool's was the first force in the North to have a **Flying Squad.**

1964: First force to use **closed circuit television.**

1981: Liverpool Police were the first force to fire **tear-gas at rioters.**

Liverpool's Crime Squad was **the first outside London to have an Intelligence Bureau.**

1956: Ivy Wood of West Derby, Liverpool becomes **the first female Police Superintendent in Lancashire.** She came to Liverpool in 1948 and rose through the ranks before her retirement in 1971.

(For further details of the history of our Police Force, the reader is recommended to read *From Cutlasses to Computers. The Police Force in Liverpool from 1836 to 1989* by W. Cockcroft. I am also grateful to Mersey-Guide Hilary Love for some of the information above.)

OTHER PUBLIC SERVICES

Gas: Shilling-in-the-slot **gas meters were first introduced in the UK by**

Liverpool Gas Company. In 1889 the first fifty meters were fitted in artisan dwellings in Cazneau Street, Liverpool – which pioneered the popularisation of gas installation in the homes of the lower income groups. The *Liverpool Mercury* of the day suggested that it was a welcome innovation and should be extended to all consumers, not just those living in houses rented at 7s.6d a week (the equivalent rent today would be about £37 per week).

Telephone: Britain's first automatic **telephone exchange** (1912) and the heart of **the country's subscriber trunk dialling system** (1958), were both produced by the **Strowger Works** in Edge Lane, Liverpool. Britain's **first automatic telephone system was produced at the same factory in 1912.**

Pillar-boxes: Liverpool was **first to introduce the little movable panels in pillar-boxes that showed collection times** (1875), but only second in the country to use pillar-boxes. The first such pillar-boxes were installed in Cheltenham in March 1854. Liverpool followed a few months later with the first pillar-box being sited near the junction of Croxteth Road and Sefton Park Road.

Salvage Corps: In 1842, Liverpool's Insurance Companies founded **the Liverpool Salvage Corps, the first in the UK.** London, Glasgow and Bombay followed many years later.

1842: Only one full-time Fire Officer – the Chief – on a salary of £150.

1865: Expanded.

1902: First motor **fire-engine in the UK.** (See also: Police)

1907: Its salvage expertise was so renowned that the Corps was once called in to deal with the aftermath of a large fire in Hamburg.

1969: The Corps was 100-strong with a fleet of ten radio-equipped vehicles.

RELIGION

Our knowledge of the ancient history of Liverpool and Merseyside is somewhat sparse, and particularly in regard to religion – in whatever ritual it was practised, be it Stone Age, Iron Age, Roman, Celtic, Saxon, Norman, or more recent. It seems to be cautiously accepted that Iron Age people travelled and settled in one or two parts, (Camp Hill, Woolton and Down-holland Moss, for example) with their own religious practices and that maybe Boat People, who lived on the seas at the western edge of Europe, may have come ashore to bury their chieftains with some kind of religious ritual (e.g. Calderstones and the Boar's Den Tumulus on Harrock Hill, Parbold). It is also accepted that Celts settled in Walton ("Wala" = *Welsh*, plus "tun" = *dwelling place* = "place of the Welsh"), leaving a round graveyard as their trademark, and in Wallasey ("wallas ea" = *the dwelling of the Welsh*). The Saxons built Christian churches on sites we can still trace such as St Nicholas's at the Pier Head, Prescot Parish Church, Kirkby St Chad's and Walton on the Hill among others. A few Norman church sites or remains are still visible and can be visited (Shotwick Church, Bebington Parish Church, Ormskirk and Birkenhead Priory).

Birkenhead Priory, home of the Benedictine monks, who started our ferries in AD1125

St Germanus is said to have preached in this area in the 5th century, and St Patrick is supposed to have sailed from Liverpool (or Wirral), before being captured by pirates and taken to Ireland as a slave. Which of these events could be considered Firsts is debatable. What has been documented is the advent of Benedictine monks to **Birkenhead Priory in 1125, where they started the ferries** – a First for the Benedictines of Merseyside. Other Benedictines (from the Abbey of St Martin de Sees in Normandy) settled at Walton-on-the-Hill (under the aegis of Roger of Poictou) after the Norman Conquest, and a further group settled at Stanlowe Abbey (on a site next to what is now the second-largest oil refinery in Europe). They found the riverside conditions too damp and cold, and eventually sought and received permission (from Father Abbot, from the Lord of the Manor of Chester and from the Pope) to establish a big abbey at Whalley in the Ribble Valley.

Walton and Childwall

We know that there were originally only two parishes in Liverpool: Walton parish which covered a huge area from (and including) Toxteth, Anfield, Aintree, Bootle and as far as Freshfield and Formby; and Childwall which included Wavertree, Halewood, Woolton, Gateacre, Hale, Garston, and Speke. To save walking five or six miles from the city in order to attend Mass at Walton, a Chapel of Ease was built at the Pier Head (St Nicholas's, today), and to save a 4-mile walk from West Derby to Walton, a similar chapel-of-ease was built at West Derby.(See more about Walton Church, below.)

The Reformation was slow to take effect in this part of the world because we were so far from the centre of operations, London. Hence, we find the Molyneux of Croxteth providing a secret Mass centre for local Catholics once the latter were forced to leave West Derby Chapel – but long after the rest of England had "conformed".

What happened afterwards, from the Reformation to the Ecumenism of today, is very well documented and widely known. Many regret much that took place or believe it is best forgotten, but thinking people hope that lessons have been learned.

Walton Church is on the site of an older Celtic settlement and church, and there is an old Saxon Font inside the church. This makes it **possibly the oldest church site within the Hundred of West Derby**. Within the church grounds a Victorian mortuary, a hearse house, a 17th century sundial and **the only Tudor Grammar School on Merseyside** can still be seen. After the destruction of the nave by incendiary bombs in WW2, the Grammar School was used for wedding breakfasts.

In the graveyard are many important tombs of prominent Liverpool citizens. One grave causes a certain amount of grim amusement. It is the grave of an actor, John Palmer, who was performing in *The Stranger* at Liverpool's *Theatre Royal* in 1798. Having just declaimed the line, " Oh God. There is another and better world.", he dropped dead on stage! **A First for excellent timing?**

Those with strong beliefs still struggle on with laudable determination. The results of their loyalty, to whatever Faith they hold dear, may not be considered by some to be earth-shattering, but they represent significant achievements. The following Firsts, therefore, though not numerous, reveal a width of distribution, throughout different creeds, places and times, that is encouraging.

1860: It was usually thought that the first **Ecumenical Conference** was held in Edinburgh in 1910. However, a book relating the life of Bishop Bell of Chichester (published by S.C.M.) recorded that the first Conference **was held in Liverpool in 1860**.

1872: "The Catholic Church built by Protestants". Under this startling headline, the *Daily Post* for 23rd November 1965 revealed that with the land being prepared for the building of the second Mersey Road Tunnel (Kingsway), the Roman Catholic Church of All Souls, Collingwood Street, was earmarked for demolition at the beginning of 1966. This church has a special place in local ecumenical history – **it was built in 1872 by Protestants in the city who were distressed by the plight of Roman Catholics** living in foul, overcrowded slums in Vauxhall.

So terribly crowded was the Vauxhall area, for Catholic and Protestant alike, that it was quite common for a whole family to eat, sleep and live in a single room – usually in one of the infamous "courts". What may not be realised is that such an overcrowded room would often also be occupied by a corpse awaiting burial. One parishioner (of All Souls, according to a parish priest there) had been found sharing her bed with the corpse of her husband for some days.

Protestant businessmen in the city were so appalled that they collected £4,970 for the building of a mortuary chapel, "which would at least enable Catholics to bring out the dead from their homes for the five or six days preceding burial." (D.P., 23rd November 1965.) At the opening of the Chapel, Liverpool's Catholic Vicar General described the Chapel as "a monument which shall continue to publicise the alms-deeds of the merchant princes of Liverpool till the last stones shall crumble into dust". This Chapel later became All Souls Church.

As related elsewhere, Liverpool can hold its head high with its fine record of Ecumenism, in and around the City, thanks to the efforts of hundreds of lay people led by Bishop Sheppard and the late Archbishop Worlock over the past twenty years or more. The most moving proof of this, in the writer's opinion, was seen the day following the Hillsborough Disaster when thousands of people, of all Faiths, gathered at the Metropolitan Cathedral (inside, and outside on the piazza) to pay their respects to the dead at a Memorial Mass. This was followed by a similar turn-out at Liverpool Cathedral the following week, with the whole clerical, political and social spectrum of Merseyside represented at the Service of Remembrance. It would be inappropriate to claim this as a first because that would appear to trivialise something that was uniquely sad and deeply personal for everyone. It is certainly a traumatic event that has left its mark.

One image, from the service in the open air on the piazza behind the Metropolitan Cathedral, will always remain with those who witnessed it. As the service was about to begin, away to the west, over the River Mersey, a lone helicopter swung in towards the city. It carried Bishop David Sheppard who had broken off his holiday to be with his people, and with his close friend Archbishop Derek Worlock, at a time of awful trial and sorrow for Merseyside. In the writer's humble opinion, that is ecumenism.

Liverpool Cathedral: *See earlier entry.*

Metropolitan Cathedral: *See earlier entry.*

1924: The **first broadcast by the Archbishop of York** was made in 1924, in Liverpool Cathedral, at the building's Consecration.

1925: Liverpool Cathedral was **the first to have a voluntary organisation dedicated to raising money for building and for the upkeep of the fabric of the building**. They were originally called, in 1925, *Liverpool's Cathedral Builders*. They were later known as *Friends and Builders of the Cathedral*. The idea inspired others to follow suit: Canterbury in 1927, York and Peterborough in 1928, and others later. Today, every Cathedral in Britain has such a support group.

1842: St Oswald's Church, Old Swan, was **the first Catholic church in the north of England, since the Reformation, to have a tower and spire built**. The first post-Reformation Catholic Archbishop of Liverpool and of the Northern Province, Bishop Brown, is buried at St Oswald's. In September 1989, the top 9.5 metres of the spire were found to have moved 26 centimetres (10.5 inches) in a gale that lashed the building. The stones were removed, carefully recut, then re-erected. The original Pugin tower was therefore lost, but it is doubtful if anybody, other than an expert, could tell the difference.

The Church achieved a very strange notoriety in 1973. Workmen were preparing to start digging the foundations for a new school when the then Parish Priest, Fr McCartney, advised them of the existence of a few unmarked graves at the end of the site. By law, bodies had to be removed for reburial before building could be begun, and the Home Secretary had to sign his approval for such exhumations. The Home Secretary of the day must have received quite a shock to discover that he had to sign for, not "several" bodies, but for 3,561 corpses! These were found, encased in coffins in fairly good condition, up to 5 metres down in the earth.

The source of such a mass burial (the coffins were buried in orderly piles) is a mystery, though opinion seems to favour one of the Liverpool cholera epidemics. About a mile down the road from St Oswald's stands a very old lock-up for miscreants, on Wavertree village green. It is known that during one epidemic at least, bodies were brought into this lock-up for storage overnight, before burial the next day. As the practice tended to be the burial of corpses on a hill or hillock well away from a village, it seems reasonable to suggest that the corpses at St Oswald's came from Wavertree. As the coffins bore no identification (and there is no other written evidence, such as a burial register), one burial expert pointed out that they must have been interred before 1840 because that was the year when compulsory registration of interments was introduced by Act of Parliament.

SCIENCE AND TECHNOLOGY

Possibly the greatest Renaissance figure connected with the advancement of science in this country was Francis Bacon. He was the founder of scientific method in England and a promoter of science. As he was MP for Liverpool, circa 1589, then he deserves mention as one of Liverpool's Firsts in science. However, whether Bacon was an assiduous MP for the Liverpool cause is not too clear, nor is there any evidence to prove he even visited the town; so, for the sake of accuracy, perhaps we are on safer ground commencing elsewhere.

Jeremiah Horrox (1618-1641) Astronomy

"Liverpool's scientific tradition dates from 1618 when Jeremiah Horrox was born in a farmhouse near Toxteth." (Chandler: *Liverpool*) Horrox showed early signs of mathematical genius by going up to Cambridge at the age of 14. He was a member of the Ancient Chapel of Toxteth whose Rector was another celebrity, Richard Mather. The latter was a Puritan minister who was very much at odds with the Anglican Church authorities for his revolutionary outlook and ideas. His sons, Increase Mather and **Cotton**

The ancient chapel of Toxteth, where Jeremiah Horrox was educated

Mather, were early Presidents of Harvard and Yale Universities in America when the family emigrated secretly to New England. (Two firsts?).

Horrox has always been regarded as a genius, and rightly so. In 1639 he accurately predicted the transit of the planet **Venus across the face of the sun** by using his outstanding mathematical ability and a special machine he had invented. By observing the solar parallax, **the distance of the earth from the sun could be calculated** – the first time it had been done on reasonable grounds using reliable calculations. It should be remembered that telescopes were in their infancy, so his success was the more praiseworthy. His instruments for measuring and observation were set up in Carr House, a Tudor house which still stands on the Leyland road (B5248), just off its junction with the old Liverpool to Preston road (A59), at Hoole. He died in January 1641, at the age of 23 – just over a year after his major discovery.

His experiment could justifiably be described as the culmination of a short lifetime of study by an inquiring and creative mind. It was an age when the prevailing astronomical ideas were those that had been held for centuries – partly through the lack of observation and experimentation, and largely through the strictures imposed by the Church on any contradiction of the old Aristotelian tenets (e.g. that the Earth was the centre of the universe). Horrox obtained a copy of Copernicus's *De Revolutionibus Orbium Coelestium*, 1530 (The Motions of the Heavenly Bodies) and, after long observation of the night sky locally, he found that the positions of the planets did not fit

Carr House, where Horrox made his observations

in with Ptolemy's idea of an Earth-centred universe – a concept that had existed for thirteen centuries. Copernicus and Kepler became Horrox's idols, and his experimental ideas were enlarged and promoted.

The transit of Venus forecast was remembered by the scientific fraternity down the centuries. It has tended to obscure other important discoveries he made:

¤   He worked out a **detailed theory of the Moon's motion (circa 1637 – 38).**

¤   He proposed that **planets exerted forces on one another** (which we now know as gravitational attraction – e.g. the Moon's gravitational pull causes our tides)

¤   He demonstrated that the **Moon's evection** (i.e. the irregularity in its motion in its orbit due to the attraction of the Sun) was regular, but differed from other planets.

¤   He produced a reasonable estimate of what is known to astronomers as **"the solar eccentricity".**

¤   He discovered irregularities in the motions of Jupiter and **Saturn.**

¤   He produced a model of **planetary motion** based on a conical pendulum. To help grasp this idea, tie a round object – say, a ball – on a length of string, hold the top of the string, and let the ball hang down, making a circular motion at the end of the string i.e. a conical pendulum. This may appear elementary today, but the reader is reminded that it cut completely across the accepted wisdom of the time to the extent of being heretical.

¤   Around 1638 he suggested an **elliptical orbit for the comet of 1577.**

¤   **Also in 1638, he began a study of the tides at Toxteth** which, sadly, was interrupted by his death in 1641. This was subsequently followed by the work of William Hutchinson and the later work at Bidston Tidal Institute.

His work was so revolutionary and precise that he was regarded by Sir Isaac Newton **as being amongst the top two or three astronomical pioneers in the country.** Horrox's *Opera Omnia* was published posthumously in London in 1690. It was **the first important scientific book by a Liverpool man** and is highly regarded by the Astronomical Society.

A memorial to him can be seen to the left of the altar in the Church of St Michael-in-the-Hamlet, Aigburth. He is buried in the graveyard at the Ancient Chapel of Toxteth – the chapel where he was also a lay preacher. Is it time for a public memorial to this long-neglected genius?

The author is moved to comment that this is another instance where we (the people of Liverpool) have allowed the work of a brilliant and innovative person to slip almost into obscurity, largely unhonoured and unsung. The author would like to think that he may have opened up thoughts about starting a movement to restore the balance of fairness and acclaim to such worthy innovators of Liverpool's past (Oliver Lodge, William Lassell, etc.). (Ref: Dr Peter Rowlands, Department of Physics, Liverpool University; Peter Aughton, *Liverpool – A People's History*, Preston, 1990; and others in LRO).

Thomas Wilkinson, circa 1756

Thomas Wilkinson was Minister at St Chad's Church, Kirkby, in the Parish of Walton-on-the-Hill, for about 30 years. "He had a strong mechanical turn of mind and **invented the gold balance,** which was once the only one in use, and which was extensively manufactured at Ormskirk and Prescot." (THSLC: Vol 6; 1853/54 page 51) He also invented several other machines which demonstrated great ingenuity. He died at the age of 65.

Warrington Academy, 1757

By the mid-eighteenth century, the spread of interest in science had been phenomenal, with great interest at all levels of society. Scientific magazines were produced, associations were instituted, and newspaper articles written. Locally, a major step was **the creation of Warrington Academy** by Liverpool and Manchester men. Marat, the French revolutionary, lectured there; and Matthew Turner taught Joseph Priestley there. Priestley, of course, earned his own first in science with **his discovery of oxygen and his invention of the "pneumatic trough".**

Rack Lever Escarpment, Peter Litherland

Peter Litherland invented and patented the rack lever escapement for watches. This permitted the energy of the watch-spring to be controlled and transmitted to the mechanism and fingers. In simple language, it was the part that made pre-quartz watches tick, literally and figuratively. His workshop stood where Lewis's Store stands today. The Prescot Watch Museum would provide the reader with very extensive detail.

William Lassell (1799-1880) – Astronomy

Those who enjoyed their post-War cricket on the local pitches of Merseyside would no doubt agree that one of the most attractive fixtures was the one against George Henry Lee's XI at Bradstones in Sandfield Park, West Derby.

It was a beautiful old house (now, sadly, demolished) in lovely grounds, and the afternoon tea they supplied for one shilling and sixpence was the best on Merseyside! On the west side of the main building used to stand a small, stone, hexagonal building with a conical roof, the use of which puzzled the writer for many years. Long after hanging up a pair of rather well-worn cricket boots, the answer to the puzzle was revealed.

One of the previous owners of Bradstones had been William Lassell, a scientist and astronomer of considerable repute in astronomical circles, who had built the conical-roofed building as an observatory and workroom. On one occasion, when Queen Victoria was staying at Croxteth Hall, he was summoned from Bradstones to the royal presence. When he arrived, the Queen rose from her chair and walked to the door of the Audience Room to greet him – an extremely rare honour.

He was born in Bolton, Lancs., on 18th June 1799, and died at Maidenhead, Berkshire on 5th October 1880. He served a seven year apprenticeship with a Liverpool merchant, then became a brewer. His mother was Hannah Gregson, of an old Liverpool family, and his father, James Lassell, also with Liverpool roots (several Lassells are recorded in Gore's *Directory* for 1825, particularly in the Toxteth area).

By the age of thirty he had made his fortune in the brewing business, so he was able, not only to afford his serious hobby of astronomy, but also to pursue lines of research and experiment that were not hindered by rigid adherence to the astronomical thinking of the day. About 1820, he began to construct reflecting telescopes, and in 1840 he installed a nine-inch Newtonian instrument in the conical-roofed workshop at Bradstones. The great **reflecting telescope**, which he later designed and built himself, eventually led to his instruments surpassing those of the great astronomer, Sir William Herschell, of fifty years before. A full-size reproduction of his 24-inch telescope was recently on view in St Michael's RC Junior School playground for a week to commemorate the great man (see also below). It can now be studied at close hand if the reader cares to visit the new Conservation Centre (in the old Great Western Railway Depot) at the corner of Whitechapel and Crosshall Street. Incidentally, **the new Conservation Centre is the only one in Europe,** and well worth visiting.

The list of Lassell's achievements is long and spectacular. Here are but a few of them:

¤   The invention and building of **a machine for polishing the reflecting "mirror"** (made of speculum metal) of a telescope.

¤   **The application of Fraunhofer's ideas** for the equatorial mounting of a telescope.

Lassell's 24-inch telescope, recently rebuilt and now housed in the new Conservation Centre

¤ The discovery of **Triton** – the larger satellite of Neptune, and **Hyperion** – the eighth satellite of Saturn in 1848.

¤ The confirmation of the two satellites of **Uranus** (Ariel and Umbriel).

He continued enlarging his telescopes, eventually constructing a 48 inch telescope with which he discovered **600 new nebulae and many new satellites.** His astronomical work, which was highly respected, resulted in the following honours:

¤ **1849: Gold Medal of the Royal Astronomical Society** (RAS), to which he had been elected a Fellow in 1839.

¤ **1870:** President of the RAS.

¤ **1858: The Royal Medal,** the medal of the Royal Society.

¤ **Honorary Member of the Royal Society of Edinburgh** and the **Royal Society of Sciences at Uppsala.**

¤ **Honorary LL.D** conferred by **Cambridge** University.

All these honours have greater significance and invite deeper admiration when it is realised that he could not go to Oxford or Cambridge as a young man because he was a Dissenter. Only members of the established Church were admitted to degree-awarding universities at that time.

He married Maria King of Toxteth whose two brothers were also amateur astronomers. Before he came to Bradstones he had lived at Starfield. The site of this building is now a school playground opposite St Michael's Catholic Church, West Derby Road, and a commemorative plaque, concerning Lassell, is being placed there by the Department of Physics, University of Liverpool.

After Bradstones he went to live in Caergwrle (to the north-west of Wrexham) before moving to Malta, where he was able to make new discoveries because of the better night sky conditions. He returned, after some time, to settle at Maidenhead, Berkshire. When he died he left a considerable fortune, amounting to between £70,000 and £80,000 – in spite of spending huge sums of money on his hobby. (These figures can be multiplied by 100 to give their approximate value today.)

His astronomical discoveries, his lens-grinding machine and his telescopes were Firsts for Liverpool, England and the World.

(Refs: several, including H.C. King, *The History of the Telescope* London, 1955; and obituaries in the *The Daily Post,* Saturday, October 9th 1880 and Monday, October 12th 1880, and *The Daily Courier,* Tuesday, October 12th 1880. Also see LRO.)

Richard Caton

1833: Caton's research into the brain led to his discovery of **electric current in the brain** - "brain-waves" in the jargon of the day. This discovery led later to the production of the **electro-encephalograph** which is such an important tool today in operations on the brain. He was a Mayor of Liverpool.

Isaac Roberts

Roberts specialised in astro-photography and made the **first long exposures of nebulae and star-clusters in 1886.** Of particular significance was a long exposure of the Pleiades which **revealed unsuspected nebulosity behind this constellation** (in Taurus). The Pleiades can be seen fairly easily on a clear night. In the same year he demonstrated that the **Andromeda nebula was a spiral nebula,** and the nearest to Earth.

(In Greek mythology: the *Pleiades* were the seven daughters of Atlas who were turned into a constellation at their death. *Andromeda*, the daughter of Cassiopeia, was rescued by Perseus from a sea monster, for whose delectation she was fastened to a rock.)

George Higgs

Higgs undertook the study of the spectra of the Sun and the stars in 1890 – pioneering work again.

First Multiple Switchboard, 1884

1884: The first Multiple Switchboard was installed in the Liverpool Cotton Exchange.(Ref: David Robinson of *Technology Response*)

James Muspratt 1793-1886 Chemical Industry

Born in Dublin, Muspratt is referred to as **the founder of the British chemical industry**. He opened an alkali works in Vauxhall Road, circa 1822, which was especially famous for its extremely tall chimney. (It proved valuable to shipping in the Mersey and the Approaches as a landmark, and was marked on the early local charts.) The overpowering smells of hydrochloric acid gas and hydrogen sulphide from Muspratt's, in conjunction with the evil emanations from other factories in the area, led to some unknown Liverpool humourist nick-naming the area, "The Spice Islands!"

Local clamour regarding the nuisance value of the factory led to a successful court indictment, and the factory had to close. Muspratts had other factories in Widnes (1870), Newton-Le- Willows and Flint. His chemical empire became part of the United Alkali Company (1890s), which in turn became part of ICI in 1926. The writer, along with other Merseysiders of his generation, well remembers a Musprattesque epithet being applied to a heavy smoker – "He smokes like a Vauxhall Road chimney". The Muspratt Building, in the original University Campus on Brownlow Hill, was erected in his honour by his family, with benefactions he had made before his death. His son was James Sheridan Muspratt.

James Sheridan Muspratt 1821-1871

Sheridan Muspratt wrote *Chemistry, theoretical, practical and analytical as applied to the Arts and Manufactures* (published Glasgow, 1860) which received world-wide acclaim. **Harvard University, USA, bestowed upon him the First Honorary M.D., ever granted to a British subject.** He returned to Liverpool to set up the Liverpool College of Chemistry in 1848, which was known in Germany as " The Great National Chemical Work".

Thomas Mellard Reade

The early Victorian period saw a great upsurge in the study of Natural History – Geology, Archaeology, Anthropology, etc. Many local people undertook very considerable and painstaking researches in all sorts of fields of learning, in the true spirit of amateurism. So expert were these researches and researchers that, in the case of Geology, their findings and comments were **incorporated in the first *Geological Survey of Great Britain* produced by H.M. Government.**

One of these unsung specialists was Thomas Mellard Reade who, in 1876-79, **extended the age of the Earth after using special techniques based on the sedimentation of rocks.** He had a big argument with the great scientist Kelvin who had opted for an Earth age of 100 million years. Reade extended this to 1000 million years and more. Modern research has proven Reade's superior capability in this geological field.

Locally, he forecast, for example, that his studies of the geology of the Mersey Estuary indicated earlier river channels beneath the bed of the river. One of these appeared to be a long and deep "lens" of clay (probably boulder clay). He was proven right when the builders of the Mersey Railway were tunnelling under the river's strata and hit a deep bed of clay. The tunnel had to be excavated at a deeper level to go under this lens.

Sir Oliver Lodge (1851-1940) Inventor of Radio

One of the greatest errors ever made, and still perpetuated, is the claim that radio was invented by Marconi. Apart from the fact that scientists do not favour the use of the word "invention", preferring "development" (which emphasises the lengthy research that must be undertaken by many researchers over a wide field before a breakthrough occurs), there is the hard evidence that the first transmission and reception of a radio signal took place in Oxford University. **The scientist who demonstrated this breakthrough was Sir Oliver Lodge.** Sir Oliver Lodge was elected **the first Professor of Physics at University College, Liverpool,** in June 1881 and was a pioneer in wireless, undertakng research into electro-magnetism and the nature and propagation of radio waves. **He coined the term "coherer"** for his very sensitive detector (wireless receiver), and was the **first person to use "syntony", as he called it, for selective tuning.**

His major feat in radio was accomplished when he accepted a challenge to provide a public demonstration at Oxford. **The first radio message, on 14th August 1894, was transmitted from the Clarendon laboratory, 60 metres (180ft) through two stone walls to the Oxford Museum lecture theatre,** before a scientific audience of members of the British Association. This must rank alongside Hertz's work of 1888 and Marconi's trans-Atlantic transmissions in 1901 (the dates are important to note) as one of the great achievements in radio.

His next (long-distance) transmission was from the top of the University Clock Tower on Brownlow Hill (the Victoria Building) to a receiver on the roof of Lewis's Store at the bottom of Brownlow Hill – **a distance of about half-a-mile.** His later frequent transmissions from the Clock Tower led to his getting into trouble with the public services. It became his practice to send a wireless message to his wife, before leaving for home in Waverley Street, advising her to begin preparing his evening meal. Unfortunately, his radio signals were setting off various alarms in the vicinity of the signals, so the practice had to cease!

Marconi's contribution was the transmission of a radio message from a ship at sea to a shore station. The value of such a transmission was obvious – to be able to call for assistance in a time of peril. The success of this first such transmission – reception caught the public's imagination and assured Marconi's success as a manufacturer of radio sets. Being not only wealthy but a very good PR man, he went on to create a thriving business.

Lodge, who fulfilled the popular image of a true Victorian scientist, with his long white beard and high-domed forehead, was more interested in research than in making money. He went on to produce the **ignition system** for the internal combustion engine and even had time to encourage his sons

Sir Oliver Lodge, inventor of radio

to form a company producing **spark plugs** – the famous Lodge Plugs. He achieved local fame in being chosen as the model for a scientist in the bronze group of figures symbolising "Learning" at the base of the Victoria Monument, Derby Square, Castle Street, Liverpool.

Other Lodge experiments (Firsts) included, in chronological order:

¤ **1883 and on:** The investigation of **electrostatic precipitation**, by which dust particles were attracted to an electrically charged plate. The idea was later used experimentally to set up large plates, electrically charged, along the banks of the Mersey to attract fog and mist particles, and so disperse the fog.

¤ **1883:** The start of his experiments on **thought transference**.

¤ **1888: Electromagnetic waves around wires.** Today there are claims that illness is being caused to people who live close to overhead power cables by the electromagnetic waves emanating from the cables.

¤ **1889:** (patented, 1897), **Radio tuning** – when you tune your transistor, your television, etc., you are using Lodge's discovery.

¤ **1892: Ether drag experiment.** A most sophisticated experiment which helped the formation of the Theory of Relativity by Einstein in 1892. (Another experiment, called **Fitzgerald's Contraction** (1889), led to the observation that objects contract under speed – an effect now explained by Relativity).

¤ **1894: The invention of the "coherer"** - the first practical radio wave detector. It was the coherer that enabled the first public demonstration of radio transmission and reception to be made at Oxford, as earlier stated. Lodge was a Professor at Liverpool University at that time.

¤ **1894:** First experiments in **radio astronomy** (10th June).

¤ **1895:** He **proposed the Joule** as the unit of heat.

¤ **1896: Pioneering work on medical X-rays** with Dr Robert Jones and Thurston Holland. The first use of **X-ray equipment in Liverpool** took place when he was asked to find a bullet lodged in a child's wrist. He found the bullet and the child's wrist was eventually healed. He made **big improvements in the design** of X-ray tubes.

¤ **1897:** The **transmission from the University** Clock Tower (see above).

¤ **1897:** He calculated the approximate **size of the electron** (12th March).

¤ **1898:** The **moving-coil loudspeaker made and patented** (24th April). This was a most important discovery because without it we would not have our hi-fi radio or record decks, etc., today.

The full list of his achievements in radio and other aspects of Science are listed in Appendix II, pages 203 to 210, in *Oliver Lodge and the Invention of*

Radio published for the Lodge Centenary in 1994, and edited by Peter Rowlands and J. Patrick Wilson (University of Liverpool). There are still a few copies available from the University – Oliver Lodge Building.

The centenary of Lodge's achievement was commemorated at Liverpool University, in the Oliver Lodge Building of the Department of Physics, by a comprehensive and fascinating exhibition of the actual "inventions" he produced. Many of these were on loan from Birmingham University. A special book (above) was produced (with chapters by some of today's eminent scientists), and Lodge's grandson and members of the Lodge family were present. (It was a matter of some pride to the writer to obtain all their autographs in his personal copy of this new book; and, as it is the only such autographed copy in existence, it must surely be claimed as the writer's own First for Liverpool!)

The accompanying illustration is of a card issued at the Centenary celebrations in a specially arranged wireless room (the Special Event Station), in the Oliver Lodge Building, by the Liverpool and District Amateur Radio Society, who operated there during the celebrations. The radio hams received hundreds of radio messages of congratulation from all over the world, to which they replied. Visitors to the Special Event Station could ask for messages to be sent or received.

The University of Liverpool

GBØOL

Special Event Station operated by the Liverpool and District Amateur Radio Society to commemorate the centenary of the transmission of the first radio message in 1894 by Sir Oliver Lodge.

— — —	• — • •	• •	• • • —	•	• — •	• — • •	— — —	— • •	— — •	•
O	L	I	V	E	R	L	O	D	G	E

Commemorative card issued by Liverpool and District Amateur Radio Society

Sir Charles Sherrington, Nobel Prize

He was President of the Royal Society and world-famous for his pioneering work, at Liverpool, on the nervous system:

¤ **1896:** Traced the **cutaneous distribution of the posterior spinal roots.**

¤ **1897: Introduced the synapse** in the brain.

¤ **1897:** Provided the classical definition of **reciprocal innervation.**

¤ **1898:** Described **decerebrate rigidity.**

¤ **1900:** Described the **motor functions of the spinal chord** – a subconscious reaction to a close external stimulus.

These discoveries may seem very abstruse to the layman (including the writer), but they have been deliberately included to show the kind of on-going research that is vitally important – just one small step for man on the long journey through a research programme. Rarely, if at all, does such minute research make the headlines or appear on TV News; yet such small steps are important Firsts in their own field.

Sir John Brunner 1842-1919

The son of a Swiss pastor, Brunner was born in Everton in 1842. He and Dr Mond became partners in the chemical industry and established alkali works near Northwich in 1873. The firm flourished and became one of the forerunners of **ICI.** In addition to representing Northwich as an MP from 1885 to 1910, he was also a patron of Chairs in Economics, Archaeology and Physical Chemistry at Liverpool University. The Mond chemical complex at Weston Point, at the head of the upper Mersey Basin, near Runcorn, is familiar to many Merseysiders.

Atlantic Cable

The first successful Atlantic Telegraph Cable was financed and made by Liverpool, and laid down by the *"Great Eastern"* in 1866. The engineer in charge was Cyrus Field

Sebastian Ziani de Ferranti 1864-1930

Ferranti was born in a house at the top end of Bold Street on the right-hand side – the building had a plaque on its wall announcing this fact until just after WW2. He was an electrical engineer and inventor, taking out **176 patents** during his life. He moved to Deptford, London, when he was in his early twenties and was responsible for **planning an electrical supply system for large areas of London north of the Thames.** (See Liverpool Heritage Walk, Plaque 17)

Frederick G. Donnan

Professor Donnan held the Brunner Chair of Physical Chemistry in Liverpool (1903 to 1913) – **the first Chair of Physical Chemistry in the UK.** He produced **the Donnan Equilibrium** which related to semi-permeable membranes. These were membranes that permitted matter to pass through them one way but not the reverse way – rather like a one-way valve. They were an important discovery in the search for a treatment for diabetes. The Donnan Laboratories are named in his honour. He left in 1913 for University College, London. (See also: Matthew Dobson, 1776, in Health.)

First Strowger Switch, 1912

The **Automatic Telephone Company (of Liverpool) installed Britain's first Strowger Switch at Epsom in 1912.** The switch was invented by Strowger in America. The story of its invention makes an intriguing tale. Strowger was an undertaker, one of two in the town where he lived. After some time, he realised that his rival was receiving all the undertaking business whereas he was getting none. He made enquiries and discovered that the rival had persuaded the lady operator at the local telephone exchange to route all calls for undertaking to him, thus cutting out Strowger! The latter sat down and thought out the details for a switch that would eliminate the operator. It was duly installed – and she lost her job! Strowger is remembered in the Strowger Works in Edge Lane, Liverpool, where trams were once made and MerseyBus buses and coaches are now garaged.

Sir Robert Robinson, Nobel Prize, 1911

Robinson's work was with **alkaloid bio-synthesis** which is concerned with describing the alkaloids and their properties. He also **synthesised tropinone.** He held the Chair of Chemistry from 1915 to 1920. The Sir Robert Robinson Laboratories are named after him.

Sir Ronald Ross

The first lecturer appointed to the new School of Tropical Medicine, and later world -famous for his **discovery of the nature of malaria and its transmission by the malaria-carrying mosquito.** For this work he received the **Nobel Prize in 1902.** (See also: School of Tropical Medicine.)

Professor Charles Glover Barkla 1877-1944

Professor Barkla was born in Widnes in 1877, and later became a product of the famous Liverpool Institute for Boys (affectionately referred to as "the Inny" by past pupils). In 1895, he went to University College (the original name for Liverpool University) where he graduated with First Class Honours in both Maths and Physics; then received his Masters Degree in 1899. He went to Cambridge to work with J.J. Thompson, investigating X-rays.

1902: He returned to Liverpool as the first holder of the **Oliver Lodge Fellowship** and started a series of experiments on the properties of X-rays. He worked in the old Physics Department behind the Victoria Building (where the University Clock-tower stands).

1904: Polarisation of **X-rays.**

1906: Characteristics of X-rays.

1906: Discovery that **the number of electrons in atoms was not thousands, as previously thought,** but only a few, and was about the same number as the atomic weight. Without this very basic research it would have been impossible to learn the secret of atomic structure, nor would there have been any advance in electronics. Modern developments, like the laser beam, have descended from this branch of knowledge.

His labours led to the award of his Doctor of Science degree in 1909, and, more importantly, the award of his **Nobel Prize in 1917.** He was Professor of Physics at King's College, London, from 1909 until 1913, when he moved to Edinburgh University where he held the Chair of Natural Philosophy for 31 years.

In gaining the Nobel Prize, both Barkla and Chadwick became Firsts in the world. (Ref: Physics Dept, Oliver Lodge Building, University of Liverpool.)

Collie's Electric Coupling, 1919

Mesrs. Hughes and Young, Patent Agents of Chancery Lane, London, granted a patent to Mr J.H. Collie, of 22, Hill Rd., Birkenhead, who **developed an idea relating to an electrical coupling for tapping into uncut, exposed electric cables.** Today motor cars use the principle (and a simpler construction) when, for instance, extra lighting cables have to be tapped into the existing car lighting system for, say, caravan or tent lights, etc. (Birkenhead *Advertiser,* 25/10/1919.)

British Interplanetary Society

In 1933, **the British Interplanetary Society, the first in the world**, was founded at 81, Dale Street, Liverpool, by six Merseyside enthusiasts. The founder was Philip Ellerby Cleator (1908-1994), described in the *Liverpool Echo* (1st November 1994) as " a writer, a rebel and a visionary". The scientific establishment was irritated by this new society. The Society's subsequent history was a story of trying to survive in the face of scientific and official scepticism and opposition.

In 1936, Cleator published his first book, *Rockets Through Space* which stimulated the imagination of the young people of the time. Very slowly, his reputation grew. He was invited to Germany, saw the march of the jackboots, and met the German rocket scientists who were taking the subject very seriously indeed and had been experimenting with liquid rocket fuels since 1930. Their names were Willy Ley, Rudolf Nebel, Klaus Riedel, and a young man by the name of Wernher von Braun. A year later, Cleator was organising the escape of Willy Ley to England – and others were soon following.

When Cleator tried to rouse interest in Whitehall, they retained their statutory position of heads in the sand. Eventually, he forced their hand by going public and they reluctantly gave permission for some rocket research – but within ridiculous and daunting limits: on a specially built range, with local police authority permission; using non-liquid fuels (i.e. only powder, like a child's skyrocket); of a safe design; the filming of the rocket to take place on approved premises specially licensed; etc., etc. The full, dismal and shameful story is told on pages 31 to 34 of Cleator's book, *Into Space*, published in 1953. Only when the value of liquid-filled rockets in killing people in great numbers was demonstrated did the hierarchy wake up. By then, German scientists were years ahead of us in rocket research.

Cleator lived in Heswall, Wirral and died in 1994. His obituary, quoted in *The Echo* (1st November 1994), was perhaps the only time many Merseysiders ever heard of him, and the final sentence of the obituary stated, quite simply, "Merseyside has lost a great man."

An earlier tribute was paid to Cleator, and to his founder members of the British Interplanetary Society, by no less a person than the great rocket scientist Dr Wernher von Braun, who was the brains behind the V2 rocket that so nearly turned the war in Nazi Germany's favour, and who ultimately became the chief scientist behind the Moon Landing project in the USA. (D.P. 15th July 1969; L'pool Echo 1st Nov 1994; and Cleator's books, already quoted.)

Sir James Chadwick 1891-1974

Chadwick attended Manchester High School. In 1908 he entered Manchester University, from where he graduated in 1911. He worked there with Rutherford, gaining his MSc degree in 1913. After internment in Germany as a prisoner during World War I, he returned to Cambridge in 1919 to work again with Rutherford on the transmutation of light elements, using alpha particles from radio-active nuclei. In 1932, he made the fundamental discovery of the existence of neutrons, which led to the award of his **Nobel Prize in 1935** (awarded after his arrival at the University of Liverpool). His **discovery of the neutron led to the fission of uranium and the creation of the atomic bomb.**

He was the Lyon Jones Professor of Physics at Liverpool from 1935 to 1948, during which time he was attached to the Manhattan project. He headed the research team which included Otto Frisch, Joseph Rotblat and others who, in 1941, established the fact that the isotope called Uranium 235 would be suitable for an atomic bomb. This team went to Los Alamos, USA, for the final tests. This eventually resulted in the bombing raids on Hiroshima and Nagasaki.

In 1946 Chadwick wrote, "Liverpool can justifiably claim to have had a direct share in the construction of the atomic bomb, and indeed a notable share, for we provided some of the ideas and some of the essential data on which depended the possibility of the bomb."

Joseph Rotblat was awarded the **Nobel Peace Prize** in **1995.**

Hyperbolic Cooling Towers

The first hyperbolic cooling towers in Britain – those giant towers shaped like cotton reels - were first erected at Lister Drive Power Station, Stoneycroft, in 1924. This discovery was made by Dr Nicholas Pevsner and was reported in the Architectural Review (circa 1969). He reported how the trail had led to Holland, to two Dutch men who had taken out a patent on such towers in 1916, but Liverpool really launched these towers.

Capenhurst

The **first plant in Europe to produce enriched Uranium** was built at Capenhurst, Wirral in 1949.

Thomas P. Hilditch

1940: Hilditch published **the classic work on the constitution of fats** – a matter of serious concern to us all these days. He held the Chair of Industrial Chemistry at Liverpool and his research concerned oils, fats and waxes.

Herbert Frölich

1950: Professor of Theoretical Physics at Liverpool University (1948 – 1973), his researches paved the way for the explanation of **super-conductors** – the new wonder-conductors which give us more power for less effort. He was already an acknowledged expert in the field of dielectrics (electrical insulators). If young readers are reading this book, they may be encouraged to enter the scientific field by learning of Frolich's early life.

At 15, he left school and travelled round the German countryside collecting folk songs. After a short time in business he decided to improve his education, and while constructing a radio receiver, he became interested in physics. After teaching himself the higher mathematics needed for University entrance, he studied theoretical physics at Munich (then the world centre for the subject).

His solution to a particularly abstract problem (the absorption of light by metals) was so impressive, he was awarded a Doctorate without even taking a first degree! Before leaving Germany in 1933, he wrote his first textbook on solid state physics (including work on semi-conductors).

He came to Liverpool in 1948 (via Bristol University) to take up the first Chair of Theoretical Physics; was made a Fellow of the Royal Society in 1951; was awarded the Max Plank Medal by the German Physical Society; became Professor Emeritus at Liverpool; and was Professor of Solid State Physics at Salford (1973-76). It was said of him that "his life was a mathematically guided tour of discovery".

Sir Cyril Clarke and Philip Sheppard

These two scientists, working in the 1960s, discovered how to **prevent rhesus haemolytic disease** – **the rhesus factor** – which could cause haemolytic anaemia or even more serious consequences. The name is taken from the small catarrhine monkey, common in Northern India. (The name "Rhesus" was arbitrarily taken from a mythical King of Thrace, in Greece – King Rhesos.)

Solar Energy

In 1961, **St George's Secondary School**, Wallasey, was opened, but this was a school with a difference. It was **heated by solar energy**. The system was designed by Wallasey's Principal Assistant Architect, Mr Emslie A. Morgan, who died in 1964. His death immediately posed a particular, urgent problem for St George's – he was the only person who knew how the school's solar system worked. Though some of his notebooks were found, their contents have not been revealed.

Of course, objections were raised based on complaints arising from existing thermal buildings: unbearably hot in summer and excessively cold in water. Interest waned for some years then, in 1975, an account of the school's solar system was given at the International Solar Energy Society's conference in Los Angeles. "It then became regarded as the forerunner of the solar houses then being built in the south-west of USA". (See article quoted below.)

The building, clearly visible from the M53 mid-Wirral motorway, has three claims to fame in the context of post-war UK architecture:

¤ It may well be **the oldest** such building in the world (in current use) which was designed to make use of what is called "passive solar gains" i.e. only the sun's heat is used without mechanical assistance such as fans or pumps.

¤ Housing 300 pupils, it is probably **the largest** in use in the world, and certainly the largest in the UK (in 1986).

¤ At latitude 53.4 degrees North, it is further north than the majority of solar houses.

¤ Emslie Morgan was in the course of patenting his design when he died. The Patent Specification appeared in 1966 (Morgan 1966).

The heat for the school is provided by solar gain through its almost entirely glazed wall that faces a little west of south. Body heat also contributes to the heat need, and the electric lights too have an effect. In short, it is a complex formula of heat sources, heat loss and heat absorption. (The above information is from *Energy Research, Vol.10*, 101-120 (1986), and was kindly forwarded to the writer by David Armstrong, General Inspector (Development), Dept. of Education, Metropolitan Borough of Wirral.)

The school is now known as Solar Campus, and houses Education Services and Social Services.

R.A. Gregory

1964: Gregory painstakingly ground down the intestines of 18,500 cattle at Liverpool's Stanley Abattoir to isolate a mere microgram of **gastrin,** a hormone which activates digestion He worked with a collaborator named Tracey. **He deserves a First for sheer effort alone!**

George Kenner, R.A. Gregory and others

1964: This team sequenced and synthesised (described) the hormone **gastrin** (See: R.A. Gregory, above).

Much of the above, as earlier noted, is highly technical and perhaps difficult to understand, but it is typical of the kind of high-level research going on at the University of Liverpool in various Departments and disciplines. That so much of this research is the first of its kind in the world, let alone in Britain, is indeed worthy of being counted proudly among our list of Firsts. (I am greatly indebted to the Department of Physics at the University of Liverpool for the information contained in most of the above section.)

SHIPPING

"No sea that is not touched by their commerce, no climate
that is not witness to their toils." (Burke)

There is an old saying, "Liverpool is the sea; the sea is Liverpool." When it
was first heard, or who said it, cannot be recalled, but it nicely sums up the
interdependence of the Port and its maritime environment. Hence, it is only
to be expected that, within the process of the emergence of Liverpool as a
first class port throughout the last three hundred years, there would be
innovations that stemmed from the solution of local problems connected
with shipping which could be applied nationally or even internationally.
The following section demonstrates the frequency and range of those solu-
tions or innovations that were connected with shipping. It includes Firsts
in the development of shipbuilding as well as other productive ideas by local
people. As with every other section in this book, it is greatly doubted that
the list will ever be complete.

The Spanish Armada – Humphrey Brooke

1588: The discovery of plans for the "invincible" Spanish Armada to sail
against England in 1588 is credited to Humphrey Brooke, a privateer and
Master of the *Relief* of Liverpool. He reported his discovery to Sir Francis
Drake himself – and the rest, indeed, is history. However, there has arisen a
rival claim for the discovery of the Spanish plans for invasion, but as this
claim was made on behalf of two other Liverpool mariners, then no harm is
done! These two claimants were Nicholas Abraham and John Lambert.

The Brooke family served Liverpool well over three centuries. Their
service included: Bailiffs, Customs Officers, an Archdeacon, a duellist killed
in 1805, brickmakers, ropewalkers (owning and using rope-walks) and
builders. One member of the family was instrumental in rebuilding St
Nicholas Church at the Pier Head in 1774; he became President of the
Infirmary (where St George's Hall now stands) and Treasurer of the Workhouse. Brooke Street and Brooke Alley are named after him. (Ref: P.H.W.)

William Hutchinson 1715-1801

Hutchinson was born in Newcastle-upon-Tyne. At a very early age he went
to sea aboard a collier as "cook, cabin-boy and beer-drummer for the men".
He enjoyed a very eventful and, eventually, a very lucrative career: first, as
"fo'c'stle man on an East Indiaman (1738-39)"; then, in 1743, as "mate on a

Bomb's tender in Hyeres Bay" (near Marseilles, in the south of France); next as commander of his own vessel at Honduras, followed by service under the great Liverpool Privateer, Fortunatus Wright. He finally received his own *letter-of-marque* in the 20-gun frigate *Lowestoft*. These were the major events in his early career.

Then occurred a particularly traumatic experience. He and his crew had to take to the lifeboat after their ship was wrecked in a storm. They ran short of food and it soon became clear that one of them would have to die so that his body could supply food for the others. Lots were cast, and Hutchinson lost. Only the timely arrival of another sailing ship saved his life. This incident entirely changed his outlook on sailing! He came ashore at Liverpool and began a very active life in the Port's affairs. In 1759 he was appointed the First Dock Master – a post he retained for twenty years. He also became Water Bailiff – an important post dating back to Norman times when the Water Bailiff used to carry an oar as a symbol of his considerable authority. Today, a silver oar is part of the Civic Regalia in our Town Hall.

During this period, his contribution to the improvement of shipping aids in the Mersey and its Approaches was outstanding, and is generally accepted as being **the first time that such work was based on sound scientific principles.** The following list of his accomplishments reveals the range and application of his ideas and skills:

¤   He kept a register of tides (1768-93) with which he could predict the times of opening of the gates of the First Dock (See: Thomas Steers, below). This led to the printing of the First **Tide Tables**, which were issued and used as soon as they were printed. These tables continue to form the basis of modern Tide Tables. His work was nationally recognised, as a recent visit to the National Maritime Museum at Greenwich revealed.

¤   He kept records of barometric pressure, weather and winds. (Another First?)

¤   He established **a chain of lighthouses** round these coasts. (A local First, but vital for shipping from all countries.)

¤   **He inaugurated a pilotage service for local waters** and the Mersey Approaches. (Pilotage was not new. It had existed from ancient times) It, too, was a local First of considerable international importance.

¤   He improved on an invention made by **Henry Ross,** a Liverpool man, in **1779.** Ross had invented a **quick-match priming** for firing large guns very quickly and more safely. The value was seen to best advantage when, for instance, a broadside was being fired in battle. In that situation speed of firing and safety were obviously key factors. A gun that misfired

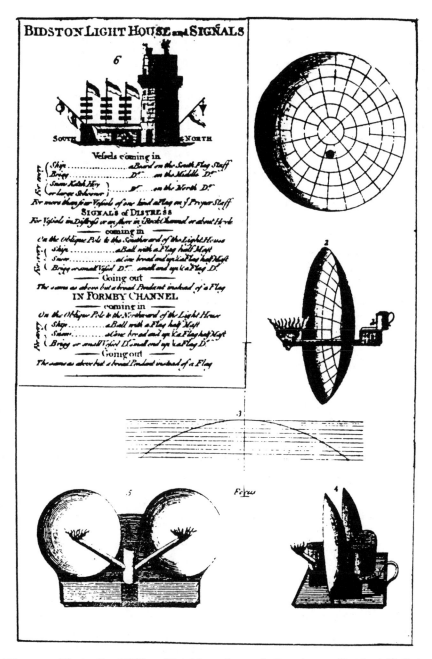

Diagrams illustrating William Hutchinson's parabolic mirrors, first installed at Bidston Lighthouse

A

TREATISE

O N

Practical Seamanſhip;

W I T H

HINTS and REMARKS

R E L A T I N G   T H E R E T O:

Deſigned to contribute ſomething towards fixing RULES

U P O N

Philoſophical and Rational PRINCIPLES;

T O

Make SHIPS, and the MANAGEMENT of them;

A N D   A L S O

NAVIGATION, in GENERAL, more PERFECT,

A N D

Conſequently leſs DANGEROUS and DESTRUCTIVE

T O

HEALTH, LIVES, AND PROPERTY.

By WILLIAM HUTCHINSON, MARINER,
And Dock MASTER, at LIVERPOOL.

P R I N T E D,
And SOLD for the AUTHOR at all the principal SEAPORTS in GREAT-BRITAIN
and IRELAND, 1777.

William Hutchinson's 'Treatise on Practical Seamanship'

or fired at the wrong time could easily spark off an onboard explosion because there was usually so much gunpowder in the vicinity.

¤ In **1763, he designed and introduced parabolic mirrors for use in lighthouses.** These consisted of small pieces of mirror set in plaster and fitted into metal bowls. He installed the first ones at Bidston Lighthouse, Wirral, and Point Lynas Lighthouse, Anglesey. The reflection of the lighthouse lamp by a parabolic mirror enabled the light to be seen further out at sea. The importance of this invention was nationally recognised and copied. Every reference book on lighthouses quotes his work in this field, and one of the original mirrors from Bidston is preserved in Trinity House, London.

¤ In **1777,** his next great work (some would say his greatest) was the production of *A Treatise on Seamanship* which included, among other important matters, methods of life-saving. With his good friend Dr Thomas Houlston, who was on the staff of the Liverpool Infirmary (on the site of the present St George's Hall), **he discovered that if apparently drowned people were taken out of the water in good time, many could be resuscitated.** (26 were saved in the initial stages of the investigation.) He submitted his ideas for artificial respiration to the Admiralty, but this august and unimaginative body rejected them. The chief consequence of their work was the establishment of the world's first **Lifeboat Station** at Formby, Lancashire. These last two achievements are outstanding Firsts.

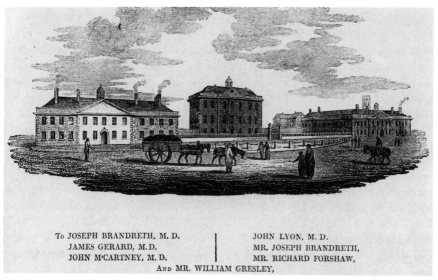

To JOSEPH BRANDRETH, M. D.
JAMES GERARD, M.D.
JOHN M'CARTNEY, M. D.

JOHN LYON, M. D.
MR. JOSEPH BRANDRETH,
MR. RICHARD FORSHAW,

And MR. WILLIAM GRESLEY,

The Public Infirmary on the site of the present St George's Hall

Incidentally, the full title of Hutchinson's *Treatise* was 65 words long! Strangely enough, such a lengthy title was not necessarily a First because long titles were the "spirit of the age" and served to emphasize the scientific importance of a work. However, it would be satisfying to know if there are longer titles than the above – just in case we have another First!

(The story of Hutchinson, and the Formby Lifeboat, is told in an excellent book by Dr and Mrs Yorke, entitled *Britain's First Lifeboat Station*. Other sources: Greenwich Maritime Museum, Liverpool Maritime Museum, and the Royal Society, Pall Mall, London.)

The First Dock

By the beginning of the Georgian period (1715-1835), Liverpool was rapidly developing in importance as a major port. Many people have ascribed this rise to the Slave Trade (1695 to 1807 in the country and colonies, but not abolished until the 1830s in Liverpool), but there was more to it than "this vile trade", as it was so aptly termed at the time.

An accident of geology (The Great Ice Age) left the port blessed with a deep, natural harbour with a bed scoured of silt twice a day by a powerful 6-knot ebb tide. Geographically, the port's position on the West coast in a corner of the Irish Sea was even more fortuitous. During the various wars with France, Holland and Spain, the south-east ports of England were virtually blockaded by the navies of these countries. However, Liverpool, being far from the European mainland, was relatively safe from attack by marauding enemy ships.

A further historical/geographical advantage became apparent as the new settlements on the Atlantic Coast of North America began to expand northwards, towards Canada. The further north they expanded, the closer they came to the ideal route to North America – the Great Circle route (used by today's airliners) – and Liverpool was best favoured for this route.

There was a human factor, too. Queen Elizabeth I granted the status of *privateer* and *letter of marque* (they were two different conditions) to many of her sea dogs. Liverpool had a fair number of these. Living in a very real and very hard commercial world, they quickly realised that risks had to be taken. One of these risks was to stop using the traditional navigational method of sailing to the Americas. This entailed sailing down a line of longitude until the latitude of their destination (say, New York) was reached, then turning west for that destination – a method used by all the major European maritime countries. The *privateers* and *letter-of-marque* owners took the calculated risk of sailing directly to the American destination using the new technology of the time – magnetic compasses, accurate chronometers and astro-navigational calculations – plus their own experience – thus saving hundreds of miles on each voyage.

There were other factors, but one very hard fact of life predominated for ships arriving here – Liverpool had nowhere to dock ships that arrived with their valuable cargoes. They anchored in the Mersey or off the North Wirral coast or in Beaumaris Bay to ride out storms; or, if they were fortunate, in the "pul" or tidal arm of the Mersey from which the port got part of its name. The low hill, on which stood Liverpool Castle (1235), gave some shelter, but at low tide ships keeled over on to their sides, unless propped up. This made unloading difficult, time-wasting and dangerous.

1708: The first rumblings of discontent from the ship owners in Liverpool were heard before 1695, but it was not until two local MPs – Sir Thomas Johnson and Richard Norris Esquire (of Speke Hall) – were asked to seek Parliament's permission to raise money for a New Dock (1708) and "to treat with and agree for a person to come to the town and view the ground and plan of the intended dock" that real progress was made. George Sorocold was approached and even supplied a design, but he died before his plan could be effected (1708). Sir Thomas Johnson eventually persuaded Thomas

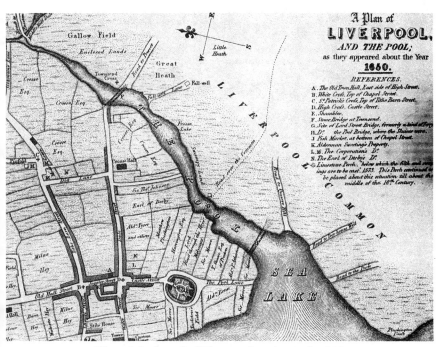

The original pool of Liverpool, as it was it 1650

Steers, who had just completed the new dock in Rotherhythe (London), to come to Liverpool and design a new dock. The Act of Parliament which authorised the new dock stipulated, "the making of a Wet Dock or Basin for the preservation not only of Merchant ships but also of Her Majesty's Ships of War." (1708) In other words, Liverpool was confirmed as a military port, which had been King John's reason for granting his Charter in 1207, 501 years before.

1719: The New Dock (later referred to as the Wet Dock and the Old Dock) was formally opened in 1719, though ships had used it since 1715. Daniel Defoe, during a visit to Liverpool, praised the New Dock. It was **the largest enclosed dock of the day**, which was later improved by the addition of an octagonal basin in the entrance leading to the main basin. The Dock had a troubled career, having to be closed to all ships for six months while the river silt was cleaned out at a cost of half-a-million pounds. No sooner was it built than it became full of shipping and it quickly became apparent that the New Dock was to be the forerunner of an expanding dock-building programme. (See: Jesse Hartley – the first enclosed dock system)

The designer, Thomas Steers, was a man of considerable talent: engineer, architect, merchant and man of affairs. As an engineer he ranks with Stephenson, Rennie, Smeaton and Brunel. He made his home here in Liverpool, was appointed Water Bailiff and Dock Master and was eventually elected Mayor. His designs for public buildings influenced Lancashire for

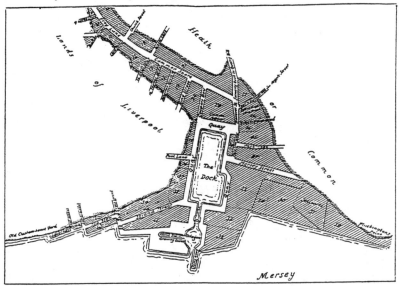

The first dock, showing land reclamation and closure of the old pool (1715)

the next forty years (First in the county?). He was also **the first to instal landmarks and marker buoys for the guidance of ships into the harbour** (which affected ships from world wide), particularly in Formby Channel which, it soon transpired, was silting up.

The accompanying illustration shows the site of the "pul" (Pool) and the land reclaimed from it to build the first dock. It quickly silted up, was later filled-in, and a Georgian Custom House built upon the site. This Custom House was damaged in the May Blitz, 1941. Regrettably, the order was given to demolish it. The site of the First Dock is now occupied by Steers House, with the new Police HQ, Canning Place, on the southern bank of the old Pool.

Lieutenant Thomas Evans

1812: Lt. Evans invented an instrument to determine a ship's position at sea by astronomical observation. He was one of several Naval men from the Georgian period onwards who charted the Mersey and its Approaches to update the accuracy of ships' charts and to forewarn of the dangers of silting and shifting channels.

Jesse Hartley – First Enclosed Dock System – Albert Dock

The greatest contribution made to the maritime development of Liverpool was by the great dock builder, Jesse Hartley. Local Merseysiders know of him because of his masterpiece, the Albert Dock, which is rightly claimed to be the "Jewel in the Crown" as Liverpool's principal tourist attraction. However, as far as cargo-handling was concerned, his greatest contribution was **the creation of an enclosed dock system of connecting docks** during his stay here as Dock Engineer, from 1824 to 1860. The significance of this is that the costliest exercises in moving ships in and around the docks were those of "locking-in" and "locking-out". It was common practice for a ship to enter one dock, discharge some cargo, then move to another dock for further discharge, and so on. Similarly, when loading-up again. To do this ships had to pass through lock gates into the river ("locking-out") then through another set of lock gates to enter another dock ("locking- in"). This cost money and time. Hartley solved the problem with the simplicity of real genius by building his dock system with connecting passages. Hence, a ship could move from dock A to dock B to dock C and so on at whatever state of the tide, without having to enter the Mersey each time – leading to a tremendous reduction in overheads and a speeding-up of cargo-handling.

Returning to the Albert Dock (opened in 1846), this noble edifice has several Firsts of its own:

¤ **The largest group of Grade 1 listed buildings in the country.** Even the dock walls are listed buildings.

¤ **The world's First enclosed dock system.**

¤ The world's first **hydraulic hoists**, designed and supplied by Armstrong's of Newcastle, were installed in the Albert Dock. Two hoists cost £1,000.

¤ **The first dock to be opened by a Prince Consort** – when Prince Albert sailed round the dock in the royal yacht *Fairy* in 1846.

¤ **The first dock warehouses built entirely of incombustible materials** – cast iron, stone, brick and galvanized iron roofing.

It is hard to resist the temptation to continue to extol Hartley's virtues and catalogue his achievements, but if the reader wishes to know more about him, there are several books available which give this information. One of these, written by MerseyGuide Elizabeth Newell, is entitled quite simply *Albert Dock, Liverpool*, and is a most useful book.

Shipbuilding Firsts

The number of Firsts attributable to shipbuilding is extraordinary; and probably the most phenomenal contributors, within this genre were the Laird family of Birkenhead. The writer is indebted for much of the following information to:

¤ *Builders of Great Ships*, produced by Cammell-Laird and Co. in 1959 (copy in the Liverpool Record Office, reference number H338.81(719) BIR)

¤ *Cammell-Laird – the Golden Years* by David Roberts (Ref. in LRO: 623.83 ROB)

¤ *Men of Iron* by D. Hollett, published by Countrywise.

All references or quotations in the following section are from the above books, unless otherwise stated. (Following this account of Laird's will be a list of other shipbuilders on Merseyside, most of whom were sited on the Liverpool side in an area now occupied by the Albert Dock and neighbouring docks. These builders are listed within their own chronology.)

William Laird came here from Scotland in 1810. "He was then 30 years old; a short, thickset Scotsman with penetrating blue eyes and an enormous zest for business." His initial task was to build up an order book for his father's ropeworks in Greenock, but the idea was a failure. Nothing daunted, he cast about for a business to create and develop. First, he became a director of two shipping companies, then he opened an agency for James Watt's steam engine, and finally he bought a sugar house.

By that time, Liverpool had rapidly ascended to a dominant position on the Mersey and in the maritime world, while Birkenhead "slumbered peacefully through the spring of the Industrial Revolution". Laird was determined to change all that. He bought land on the Wirral bank of the Mersey, intending to create a great harbour there and also drive a canal across the Wirral to link into the Dee, away from the shifting sandbanks of the Mersey and its Approaches. (This Dee harbour was to be built at Dawpool, near Thurstaston Hill.) This first purchase was on the north side of Wallasey Pool, where there was a wooden jetty called Vittoria Wharf.

Obviously he needed money, which meant that he needed partners; but neither was forthcoming. He changed course and built a boiler-making works called the Birkenhead Iron Works (1824). The idea of a port at Birkenhead collapsed, but he was already established on the Wirral and was building a town for his workers, with wide streets, an elegant square, and **gas lighting and water supply in every home** – the first two such services to be supplied to working class homes. "Several years ahead of those other industrial utopias which are credited with the origin of town planning".

He was deeply concerned with the welfare of his workers, and "appreciated the dignity of labour". He named Hamilton Square after one of his wife's ancestors who had been an Archbishop of Scotland, and he built his home in Cathcart Street, named after the house where he spent his childhood in Greenock.

1828: Laird received his first order for a vessel – a 30 metre iron lighter for the Irish Inland Steam Navigation Company (IISNC), which was completed in 1829. After a trial run, it was dismantled and shipped over to Ireland where Lairdsmen re-assembled her. She was called the *Wye*; and was such a success that two more were ordered by the IISNC. A further order from this company, in 1830, did much to establish Laird as a shipbuilder. This was the *Lady Landsowne*, a 35 metre paddle steamer, **the first to be fitted with watertight bulkheads.** It was another of Laird's ideas, and she was a beautiful ship.

If necessity is the mother of invention, then Laird's, about this time, entered into a period of necessity that engendered a long list of inventiveness. The necessity arose from the deeply-rooted opposition to iron ships by underwriters, private shipowners and Government Departments. With hindsight it is obvious that shipping was more than ready for iron ships at that time, and for several good reasons:

¤   Wooden ships had depleted the forest reserves. Forest after forest had been stripped, but farmers were not replanting woods because profits from crops were higher.

Birkenhead ironworks, where William Laird built his ships (mid-19th century)

¤   Wood for wooden ships tended to be provided in short lengths, which
    meant more joints, therefore more points of structural weakness, and
    more weight.

¤   The thickness of a ship's timbers took up valuable cargo space.

¤   Timber had to be imported, and such timber tended to be of inferior
    quality.

¤   Iron was plentiful in Britain.

1832: MacGregor Laird, while tracing relics of the explorer Mungo Park up
the River Niger in Africa, realised the potential for **trading posts on African
rivers** and set them up. He foresaw that by bringing ships up these rivers,
the prosperity of the natives could be increased by trading their produce for
the amenities of civilisation. With typical Laird idealism he was helping to
counteract the effects of slavery. He travelled up the Niger on his ship, the
Alburkah (**the first iron ship to make an ocean voyage**). The ship was
wrecked in the river.

   Another Laird ship, *Dayspring*, was also wrecked during this period of
activity in Africa, and its engine salvaged by the natives. This was fortunate
because it was **the first ship's engine to be built at Birkenhead.** It was later
displayed on Lagos Railway Station.

Laird sought other ways of changing the minds of those in opposition to iron ships. The following lengthy list of accomplishments includes many Firsts, but, more importantly, illustrates the imagination, scientific application and determination of Laird to establish and develop his shipbuilding yard, and his equal determination to establish iron ships.

1834: The *John Randolph* built – **the first iron ship to be built for a North American owner.**

1837: The completion of the then largest-ever iron ship for the General Steam Navigation Company.

1837: The chief argument from the anti-iron lobby was concerned with the effect that iron had on a ship's compass – an effect called deviation. Wrecks due to compass problems were both considerable and catastrophic. Typically, Laird tackled the problem head-on. He invited the Astronomer Royal (Professor Airey) to help solve the problem by carrying out tests aboard the *Rainbow*. These tests were rewarded with a remarkably favourable discovery – namely, that an iron ship, being iron all round, did not have the same effect on a compass as that of an iron object (e.g. cargo) being moved about in a wooden ship. Both caused deviation, but the "misdirection of the iron ship was constant", so it could be corrected. The anti-iron opposition remained stubbornly unimpressed.

The problem was eventually solved by the addition of two massive iron balls, one on either side of the binnacle which contains the ship's compass on the ship's bridge. These two spheres could be adjusted, to left or right, when the ship was "swung" to correct its compass. This invention, plus the binnacle lantern, were credited to John Bywater (1921), a Liverpool man (ref: P.H.W.). The place where compass "swings" were carried out could be seen, until recently, from the Mersey Ferry. After leaving the Landing Stage, and passing *HMS Eaglet*, there used to be a long dock shed on the sea wall. Painted on the side of this long shed could be seen faded white squares, diamonds and several compass headings – for example, 90, 95 etc. When the ship's bow was pointed at these headings, the ship's compass would be checked to see if it gave the correct reading. If not, the iron spheres would be adjusted until the correction was made and a record was kept of the deviations on main headings. Sadly, this very important piece of maritime archaeology has been demolished for new dockside development.

1836: (For the **first iron ships to be surveyed by Lloyds of London**, see Other Liverpool Shipbuilders.)

1838: *Robert F. Stockton* – **the first screw-driven ship.** Laird's, at that time, were helping the East India Company to explore a short sea route to India.

The route taken was by Laird-built ship to the Eastern Mediterranean, overland to the Persian Gulf, then on the Laird-built *Euphrates* to India. Laird's also built *L'Egyptien*, **the first iron steamer to make passage from England to Alexandria and then up the Nile.**

By 1838, Laird's had built 17 iron ships, but economic conditions became unfavourable, competition stiffened and orders fell off. A slump overtook Birkenhead; gas to houses was cut off and weeds began to push up through the cracks in the pavements. There was even talk of closing the shipyard. Laird struggled on patiently.

1840: The first iron steamship to be owned by the Admiralty was Laird-built – the 35 metre packet-boat *Dover*. Launched in May 1840, she weighed 228 tons with a 7 metre beam. (Ref: Laird Company Magazine, *The Camel*, November 1919 edition, p.8)

Four gunboats were built for the Admiralty and used in China during the First Opium War. One of them (appropriately named *Nemesis*) was so successful that she was known as "The Devil Ship" to the Chinese. She was **the first iron ship to round the Cape of Good Hope.** Resulting from the success of *Nemesis* came an order for four gunboats for the Admiralty in 1840.

1842: The **first iron lightship**, the *Prince*, was built to replace the North West Light (the most important navigational aid in the Mersey Approaches). It lasted until 1896. Up to this time, wooden lightships had been used, following the earlier use of floating lights (some constructed with a barrel, some of cane basketry).

1850s: The long-awaited golden age dawned at last, thanks to the removal of the **Navigation Laws.** These controversial laws stipulated that British goods must be carried in British ships manned in no less high proportion by British seamen. At first sight, a good idea for shipbuilders, shipowners and crewmen, but it led to a deadly complacency. When, eventually, the shipowners looked closely at their shipping stock they found the ships to be corrupt, obsolete and shoddy. Suddenly, there was a wide, almost panic-stricken, demand for new ships.

The Admiralty continued to argue against iron ships, deeming them only suitable for river work and short sea voyages. Laird decided to try and change their opinion by building Ship No. 42 "on spec". It was a 60 metre frigate propelled by paddle wheels – still preferred by Naval critics to the new ship's "screw". It was rejected by the Admiralty and sold to Mexico where it was named the *Guadalupe*. It won several sea-fights in the Mexican War against Texas and thereby proved its usefulness and safety.

Another frigate was built – the famous *Birkenhead*. She had her guns removed before sailing to the Cape of Good Hope, to experience both fame and extinction. She was the ship which achieved fame by the creation of the famous "**Birkenhead Drill**" for abandoning ship – "Women and children first".

Iron ships came into their own when it was realised that they were far stronger than wooden ships, especially in bad conditions of wind and sea. A helpful incident occurred when Brunel's *Great Britain* ran ashore on the Irish coast and suffered severe battering by the sea for over a year. Amazingly, when she was eventually examined, she was found to be structurally intact, and only minor repairs were needed. Reaction to this kind of evidence was swift and at the highest level.

1856: Lloyds of London acknowledged the existence of the iron merchantman and issued specifications for it.

1858: John Laird was appointed Government nominee to the newly-formed Mersey Docks and Harbour Board.

1858: David Livingstone's ship, *Ma Roberts* (the name given to Mrs Livingstone by the Africans) was built – **the first riveted, all-steel ship.** It predated the first steel ship built on the Tyne by one year. Livingstone stayed with Laird at 63, Hamilton Square, Birkenhead, while the ship was being completed. It is interesting to note that Stanley, very soon afterwards, stayed with his uncle in Roscommon Street, Liverpool, before setting out to search for Livingstone.(There was a plaque on the house celebrating this fact until its removal several years ago. It has never been found.)

The *Ma Roberts* was launched on 6th March 1858. She was immediately dismantled and shipped out to East Africa in sections aboard the sloop *Pearl*. She was re-assembled and launched on the Kongone tributary in May 1858. By the time the expedition had reached the Kebrabasa Rapids, the *Ma Roberts* had been renamed, by the long-suffering crew, the *Arthritic*, "from the puffing and groaning with which she managed her six or seven miles per hour, being easily passed by native canoes!" Her steel plates constantly leaked. Continuous repairs kept her afloat until 20th December 1860 when she ran aground on a sandbank above Senna.

A new Laird yard was constructed between Monks Ferry and Tranmere Pool. When ship-building commenced there, the emphasis changed from lighters to steamers: P&O ordered *Nubia* and *Persia*, both 14-knot steamers; cross-channel steamers were constructed for the Holyhead-Dublin and Dover-Continent crossings; **iron steamers were built for the South American trade;** and dredgers for the **East India Company.**

1860: The Institute of Naval Architects was founded. Science had arrived as the *sine qua non* for iron ship building, and scale drawings and models became the order of the day. This innovation later led to **the finest collection of ship models in Britain**, in Liverpool Museum. Each had been donated by a shipping company. The author and school friends spent many happy days in the museum before World War II, gazing in awe at the beauty and workmanship of these scale models. Fortunately, they survived the Blitz. Many are still in safe storage and others are on display in the Maritime Museum and sundry shipping offices.

1860: The City of Dublin Steam Packet Company had had three new iron ships built – Ulster, *Munster* and *Connaught* - with a top speed of 18.5 knots. These were re-engined and fitted with **new boilers with forced draught.** This increased the speed to 20.5 knots. When it was suggested that these three ships, together with the *Leinster* – the fourth member of the fleet – be equipped with **twin screws** to attain speeds from 23 to 27 knots, the General Post Office (which used them for carrying mail) settled for a 23 knot rating.

1861: William Laird retired from the shipyard and became a Member of Parliament. He died in 1873 after a riding accident. It was the end of an epoch. His sons – William, John and Henry – took over at Birkenhead. They must have been deeply impressed by the spontaneous turn-out of Laird's workmen who joined the funeral cortege on foot to pay their last, sincere tribute to a man for whom they had the deepest respect. Laird had always fostered a close working relationship with his men.

1874: The 1,588 ton turret vessel, *Los Andes*, was launched on 29th October 1874.

1877: *Isabella* – **the first steel ship for general service.** In the same year, *Storm Cock* was launched – **the first of the famous line of towing tugs, Cock Tugs Ltd.**

Laird's built 270 vessels between 1870 and 1900, including the 1,823 ton *Valiant*, built privately for the American millionaire, W.K. Vanderbilt (**a First for privately-built ships**). Between 1885 and 1900, a great deal of building was undertaken for the Royal Navy, including:

¤ *Royal Oak* (14,150 tons), *Mars* (14,900 tons), *Glory* (12,950 tons) and *Exmouth* (14,000 tons).

¤ Torpedo boats. The first was *HMS Rattlesnake* (1886*)*, **an experimental, 65 metres (200ft) torpedo-boat catcher**. It proved to be a good scouting vessel, but too slow for anything else.

¤ In 1893, *HMS Ferret* and *HMS Lynx* were launched as torpedo-boat destroyers, both much faster than *HMS Rattlesnake*. (*Lynx* was 4582 hp, whereas *Rattlesnake* was only 2700 hp.) The design was good and the rate of production reached **one vessel per 100 days** – a record for the time.

¤ In 1899, *HMS Viper* and *HMS Cobra* were built. It used to be said, about that time, that "Laird's yard without a warship was like a church without a steeple". (Sadly, in 1994, the Laird "church" lost its "steeple" for good).

By this time (late 1880s) Laird's yard had proved its worth both in numbers and quality, but had nearly overlooked a most important trend – ships were getting bigger. Laird's had not kept pace. A new yard was built at the south end of the Laird's complex – a 98.5 acre site, including a 15 acre fitting-out basin which was **the largest private wet dock in the UK** and 6 new slipways of 330 metres (1,000ft) each.

1897: First turbine driven vessel, *Turbinia,* was launched and was a great success. Patented in 1894 (Patent Number 394), she was the **first vessel to be propelled by means of a steam turbine actuating a propeller, or paddle shaft, directly or through gearing.**

1903: Charles Cammell and Company, a large steel-producing company founded in 1828, united with Laird to form the now legendary Cammell-Laird Shipbuilding Yards – a name deeply embedded in the Merseyside memory. Cammell had been experimenting with armour-plating since 1861 so the large-scale use of steel was not new to him, but it was a valuable expertise to bring to the new partnership, as the following events quickly showed.

1908: An 8,590 ton sand pump dredger (as opposed to a bucket dredger) was built for the Mersey Docks and Harbour Board (MD&HB). Named the *Leviathan,* it was one of the most memorable sights on the river and was **the biggest dredger in the world when launched** by Cammell-Laird. She could carry 10,000 tons of silt each trip and made four trips per day, lifting silt from 23 metres (70ft) below the surface. She carried two complete crews on board, with two further crews ashore so that she could work continuously. She also had four captains – two on board and two ashore. The number of crew members was 44. She was very powerful, with **a pair of giant triple-expansion engines,** and she was nick-named both *Levi* and *Scouse Boat!*

1909: *Highland Laddie* – a 7,117 ton passenger and chilled-meat ship for the Nelson Steam Navigation Company (NSNCo) - **the first time this combination had been built.**

1912: The largest floating dock in the world, 49,000 tons and a legend in its own time, was built at Laird's then towed to Portsmouth by the famous Cock Tugs for the Admiralty. She was 225 metres (680ft) long, 48metres (144ft) beam, and a depth of 22metres (65ft 6ins). She could lift 32,000 tons.

1913: The launch, on the 11th of March, of the *King Orry* for the Isle of Man

***Leviathan*, the biggest dredger in the world, launched 26/10/1908**
(Williamson Art Gallery and Museum)

Steam Packet Company (IOMSPC) – a ship still spoken of with great affection on Merseyside. During its long life it must have carried hundreds of thousands of motor-cycle enthusiasts over to the Isle of Man for the famous TT Races – surely a First within Europe at least! (See below, also, under World War I)

1914: Nine months after the *King Orry* was launched, the **ice-breaking train ferry** *Leonard* was launched (17th Jan 1914). It was an immense, highly technical and highly specialist vessel for use on the St Lawrence River in Canada by the Canada Trans Continental Railway. The motive behind this vessel was typical of the time – competition between the Canadian Trans Continental and the Intercolonial Railways. The key to success would be a bridge over the St Lawrence River to shorten the journey, but such a bridge had not then been built so the *Leonard* was ordered as an ingenious stop-gap until a new bridge became a reality. There is a magnificent model of it in the Williamson Library in Birkenhead which the reader is strongly recommended to visit because no words could adequately describe the complexity of the design. It is superb. The vessel was later sold to Shell Oil Company who converted it into an oil tanker, in which role it ended its days.

1913: (July) Much experimental work with submarines resulted in the first **submarine** *(E41)* along with seven more subs (see also *Resurgam*).

1913: *HMS Chester* launched. It took part in the Battle of Jutland (WorldWar

The train ferry *Leonard* built for the Canadian Transcontinental Railway, launched 17/1/1914 (Williamson Art Gallery and Museum)

I) and gained the great distinction of seeing its youngest crew member, **Jack Cornwell, given a posthumous V.C.** for standing by his gun and keeping it firing in spite of being mortally wounded. The Boy Scouts Association have always regaled new members with this heroic story as an outstanding example of selflessness and service to one's fellow-men, and there is a Cornwell Award.

The First World War also witnessed several interesting conversions of Laird-built ships. *King Orry*, converted as an armed boarding sloop, **led the surrendered German Fleet into Scapa Flow when hostilities ended.** A contemporary oil painting of this unique event hangs in the Head office of the IOMSPC in Douglas, Isle of Man. The liner *Campania* and the IOMSPC ferry, *Ben My Chree* (another vessel held in affectionate esteem by Merseysiders), were both converted into **the first sea-plane carriers** in WWI. *Campania* was later converted for two more roles: as a floating exhibition ship for the Festival of Britain in 1951, then as the observation ship for British members of the Nuclear Physics team monitoring the exploding of the first British atomic bomb in the Pacific.

1919: Patent Application No. 32,530 made by Camell-Laird on 29th December for **ship's bulkhead doors.** These could be closed, in the event of accident (e.g. collision) to minimise flooding.

1920: *M.V. Fullagar,* built for the Anchor-Brocklebank Line, was the **first electric-welded, self-propelled, rivetless vessel**. She successfully underwent trials in March 1920, and was launched on 2nd May that year. She was specially mentioned in Lloyd's Report. She was (50 metres) 150ft long and had an interesting career. In 1920 she worked for the Anchor Line as a coaster for a year. She was then sold to the IOMSPCo., and renamed *Cavia.* She traded with Liverpool up to 1926 when she was sold to the British Columbia Cement Company Ltd. of Vancouver. This time she was renamed *Shean.* On October 20th 1930 she struck a rock off Victoria but even though loaded with 10,000 bags of cement, she did not sink. She owed her survival to one fact – she was all-welded. Had she been riveted, the shock would have "started" the rivets and she would have sunk. Thus, she had proven the value of all-welded ship construction. During the Great Depression she was laid up, being eventually sold to a certain Senor Rodriguez who renamed her *Cedros.* During the 1930s she traded round California (she was registered at Ensenada in Lower California). There is considerable mystery, intrigue, and conjecture about what her exact task was for her owner, Senor Rodriguez! In 1937, on the 31st August, she hit the M.V. *Hidalgo* and sank. (Ref: *Men of Iron*, page 32; and *Camel*, 1920, page 9.)

1920: This could be claimed to be a vintage year. **The first purpose-built "banana boat"** (built for the banana trade), the *S.S. Zent,* was launched on 1st April 1920 to handle the rapidly increasing trade in this commodity. The first load of bananas was claimed to have been distributed to Merseysiders, but they were not very impressed with the new fruit. Perhaps the price put them off. It was so high that one comment made, and reported in a local newspaper, was, "bananas are for the classes – not the masses".

1920: (April) Signor Marconi's ship, *Elettra,* refurbished at *Laird's,* started on her voyage of "electrical discovery". Formerly the *Rovenska,* she was built in 1904, by Ramage and Ferguson of Leith, for an Austrian, Dr Waechter. She was confiscated at the start of WW I.

1922: Keel laid of *HMS Rodney,* **the largest and most powerful battleship in the world**. She cost £7 million and took five years to build. She was launched in December 1925 by Princess Mary who perhaps initiated the worrying practice of having trouble with the bottle of wine when launching a ship. (See *Ark Royal* below). The bottle failed to smash the first time she swung it and she completely missed the ship the second time! A wag in the crowd called out, "Third time lucky", which proved to be an accurate prophecy!

The *Rodney* was a formidable warship. She could hurl a shell of 2,340 pounds over 20 miles, and the total weight of one of her broadsides was ten tons. She distinguished herself in World War 2, being involved in the sinking of the Bismark in 1941.

1922: Underground trains were inaugurated in London, and Laird was asked to supply **the automatic steel sliding doors for tube trains on the Piccadilly Line.**

1935: The *Ark Royal* **was the largest vessel, designed and built as an aircraft-carrier, ever to be launched on the Mersey, up to that time.** The launch did not succeed without incident – nor without typical Liverpool humour again. The honour of launching was given, on this occasion, to Lady Maude Hoare, wife of the First Lord of the Admiralty. She held the bottle of Empire Wine and swung it with considerable force at the bows of the ship. Nothing happened. She tried a second time, with even more vigour and determination – still nothing happened; and even a third time, without effect. Whereupon, a wag in the crowd called out, "Give it to Dixie!"

The reference was to the then doyen of footballers nationally, and the idol of Evertonian football fans especially, Ralph "Dixie" Dean of Everton F.C., who also made his own mark in history with a still unbeaten record. (See: Sport / Entertainment). Lady Maude thereupon swung for the fourth time, and the bottle smashed against the side of the ship. There were those on Merseyside who, with hindsight, saw special significance in this event. During WW2, the infamous traitor Lord Haw-Haw, of German radio fame (of "Reichsender Bremen, Hamburg, and the short-wave transmitter, DJA," in his own words), declared the *Ark Royal* to be sunk on at least four occasions! The same slipway was used, immediately after the launch, for the laying-down of the keel of the new *Mauretania*. The *Ark Royal* was not the first purpose-built aircraft carrier. That honour fell to Elswick's *Hermes*, which was laid down in 1919 and completed in 1924 in the south of England.

The list of renowned Laird ships seems endless, including two of immortal fame: the giant battleship, *Prince of Wales* (sunk by a Japanese aerial torpedo in the Far East in WW II); and the *Thetis*, the submarine that came to such a tragic end in Liverpool Bay while on diving trials, in 1939. She was raised, refurbished, and went to war as *HMS Thunderbolt*. She was lost in the Mediterranean while on patrol. A local paper referred to her as "the ship that died twice." Her end in Liverpool Bay was so horrific (and so contentious) that **she has earned her own First** – and, it is to be hoped, a Last – **an end to the official incompetence that caused such a lethal outcome.** (Three terrible tragedies are inscribed in the hearts of older Merseysiders: the Liverpool May Blitz, the Battle of the Atlantic and the loss of the *Thetis*. These three radio topics prompted more phone calls and letters to Radio Merseyside than any other.)

1959: On June 3rd, the Queen Mother launched RMS *Windsor Castle*, 37,639 tons, belonging to the Union Castle Line. **She was the largest ship of her kind to have been launched since WW2, and the largest ever built in an**

English shipyard. 2-shaft machinery was installed, producing 45,000 horse-power – the largest ever put into a merchant ship.

1962: The *C.S.Mercury* was launched on 20th July 1962. She was **the world's fastest cable ship** and was owned by Cable and Wireless Ltd.

Other Merseyside Shipbuilders

Before 1763, no shipyard, as such, existed on the Liverpool side of the Mersey. An early print (Buck's sketch of 1728) shows shipbuilding being carried out on the strand or foreshore, which became covered at high tide, where the Pier Head buildings stand today. John Okill (circa 1630) actually built one or two small ships on land, then launched them by pushing them off the Old Dock wall. About this time, the first shipyard (Mercer's) was probably built, though no clear idea of its site has been ascertained to date.

1782: Grayson's yard launched *Ceres* (32 guns) on which Nelson served, before it ended up as a commerce raider.

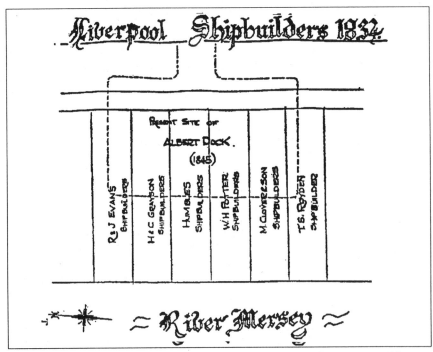

1834 map of early shipyards on the Liverpool side of the Mersey, with reference to the present Albert Dock. This was derived from a computerised scan of the only existing copy of the original map.

1819-1839: The following yards appear on local Liverpool maps: Humble and Mylchreest, Thomas Wilson, Clarke, Clover, R&J Evans, Forrester & Co., Royden, WH Potter, and Jackson. About this time, Liverpool Corporation ordered more docks to be built, which put an end to shipbuilding on this side of the Mersey, until around 1900 when Grayson's built a yard at Garston.

1820: William Fawcett, Liverpool, engined **the first steamer built in Britain to be ordered by a foreign nation.** His ship-yard was in York Street. Fawcett's continued to trade in Bromborough as Fawcett Preston. They were also renowned for producing **the first rifle to fire a shot in the American Civil War** (and, quite possibly, the last shot too, for they supplied their rifles to both sides). Liverpool people usually referred to the Duke Street firm as "Fossets".

1822: Fawcetts produced the engine for the first steamer on Lake Geneva.

1828: Fawcetts also engined P&O's first steamer, the *William Fawcett*.

1834: A map drawn in this year showed seven yards in existence in Liverpool: Baker's, Barton's, Grayson's, Fisher's, Mercer's, Rogers', and Sutton's.

1836: Fawcetts built the 77-ton ketch, *Goliath*, for dredging work in the Bay of Tunis. It was **the first iron vessel to be surveyed by Lloyds of London.**

1838: The first iron sailing-ship to be registered by Lloyds was the 270-ton *Ironside*, built by Jackson and Jordan of Liverpool.

1840: First trans-Atlantic Royal Mail service, Liverpool – New York. (See *Britannia*, below)

Britannia, 1840

The opening of the first regular steamship mail service between Liverpool and New York was accomplished by the Canadian, Samuel Cunard, in 1840. His success in gaining the Royal Mail contract assured the success of the venture, and we know, with hindsight, how successful the Cunard Steamship Company became. His accomplishment is commemorated at the Pier Head by the beautiful Cunard Building, a replica of the Farnese Palace in Rome.

The illustration shows that the *Britannia* was equipped with sail and steam. The use of both types of motive power involved a complicated procedure. The *Britannia's* captain was issued with a set of operating tables which laid down the amount of sail to be carried in various conditions of wind and current – both force and direction. In times of calm or of strong

***Britannia*, which operated the first Royal Mail steam service to New York**

headwinds, use might be made of steam power. Occasionally, conditions
called for the use of both. The Captain's decision to use either or both
systems was based on these complicated tables. A very delicate balance had
to be maintained, dominated by economics; fuel (coal) costs were high and
coal was a substantial part of the ship's cargo. Using more coal could mean
lower profits because of the necessity of carrying a lesser quantity of
profitable cargo. It was an extremely complicated exercise.

When the ***Queen Elizabeth II* came to Liverpool in 1992 to celebrate 150
years of the Cunard Steamship Company**, it was fascinating to watch the
men in the bows of this huge liner directing her slowly to her anchorage
against the incoming tide. When the pointed bow of the *Q.E.II* was dead in
line with the Cunard Building, the ship's anchor was dropped. Whereupon,
10,000 blue and red balloons (presumably equal in number) were released
by the Captain. Being a local man, he appreciated the importance of Merseyside's greatest religion – football! Needless to say, it was virtually a public
holiday and a day of celebration along the Liverpool waterfront. Her musical
departure that evening was most moving. **(A memorable First for Merseyside.)**

First Across the Atlantic in Steam, 1833

The Canadian-built paddle-steamer, *Royal William*, was the **first steamship** to be fitted with watertight compartments, which were built in Liverpool. It was also **the first steamer to make the transatlantic crossing from Liverpool to New York wholly under power.** It took 19 days on the outward journey from Nova Scotia (17/8/1833) and only 14.5 days inward (4/9/1833). It stopped occasionally for the scraping of the boilers to be undertaken! However, much of the crossing was done under sail. Perhaps this underlines the outstanding achievement of successive *Britannia* skippers (see above) in using both kinds of power (steam and wind power) so successfully.

Prefabricated Ships

Henry Kaiser, the American shipbuilder, made history (and helped to save our bacon, literally) when he constructed merchant ships in sections, often miles away from their assembly point, during WW2(1939-45). However, 150 years earlier, Merseyside shipbuilders, **Humble and Hurry, built two ships for the East India Company using timber from woodlands on the banks of the Trent and Mersey Canal at Wolesley Bridge, near Stafford.** Local oak was in short supply; and part fabrication took place at Wolesley Bridge.

Gas Illumination on Ships, 1872

The Liverpool-owned, White Star ships, *Adriatic* and *Celtic*, were **the first to be illuminated throughout by gas.** It was not a successful experiment because after a short use gas pipes began to fracture due to the ship's vibrations. Ultimately the gas system, including all piping, had to be removed.

The Mystery of the Missing Submarine, 1879

The Rev George W. Garrett, an Irishman, was born on 4th July 1852, the son of a Manchester Rector. He was a quick-learning scholar in a wide range of subjects – science, art, geography, maths, chemistry – and gained a BA from the knowledge he acquired at South Kensington Science Museum. He finally studied Theology and passed the Cambridge Theological Examination, resulting in his ordination by the Bishop of Manchester. He later became a Birkenhead curate.

During the early 1870s, Russia was at war with Turkey and it was reported that a Russian torpedo-boat commander had made an attack on a Turkish "Ironclad" – a very heavily armoured battleship. The torpedo-boat became entangled in a protective maze of chains hung over the side of the Ironclad and was, presumably, sunk (*Manchester Courier*, June 1877). Garrett read

Resurgam, the first steam-driven submarine

about this and remarked, "Why could not the attack be made by going under the chains?"

The idea of a powered submarine was born, and **in 1879 a pioneering steam submarine was designed** by this inventive Irish clergyman. He formed a limited company, including his father (2,000 shares) and J.T. Cochrane, who owned the Britannia Iron Works, an engineering and shipbuilding yard in Duke Street, Birkenhead (later to become the famous Cochrane Boilers of Annan in Scotland).

After several experiments, a cigar-shaped, steam-driven, 40ft (13 metres) boat with a conning tower was built by Cochrane's. It was launched from a 60-ton crane into the **Great Float, Birkenhead, at half past two in the afternoon of 26th November 1879.** She was called the *Resurgam*, which turned out to be a rather unfortunate choice of name because "resurgam" is the Latin for "I will rise again". The *Resurgam* was still being sought in late 1996! (However, see end of this account.) She had a 9ft (3 metre) beam and a 30 tons displacement, and was powered by a Lamm steam engine which relied on a store of compressed steam. To have used coal firing underwater would have presented many problems, not the least being the using up of oxygen. Her one boiler drove a single screw (propeller) and the whole mechanism would give her an underwater range of about 12 miles – according to Garrett. Her trials in West Float began a week later.

On the evening of 10th December 1879, this revolutionary submarine left the Mersey en route for a major trial run, before proceeding to Portsmouth where she would have to impress the Admiralty. She was crewed by Rev Garrett, Captain Jackson (a Master Mariner) and engineer George Price. They left Alfred Dock at 9 pm, rounded Perch Rock Lighthouse into Rock Channel then made for the Horse Channel which, when cleared, would mean that they were out into the open sea. They made for the North West Light where they intended to undertake some experiments in the Victoria Deep as soon as daylight broke the next day. Garrett said that the trip, so far, had gone well, commenting, "The seas passed easily over her and (there was) hardly any motion."

However, fog came down and caused further delay. Practice exercises were undertaken. On Friday morning, the sun rose beautifully clear. By this time they had been 36 hours at sea, mostly spent underwater with an inside temperature from the Lamm Boiler of over 100 degrees Fahrenheit. There was also a leakage of compressed air which hurt their eardrums – and they were completely lost, thanks to fog that had come down. Garrett hailed a passing sailing ship whose Captain directed them towards the River Clwyd – but not before he had commented, "You are the three biggest fools I have ever met!"

They eventually anchored at Rhyl for the night. The next day Garrett discovered that several mechanical parts were defective. He realised that the *Resurgam* would have to be towed round to Portsmouth for safety's sake, as well as to make up their lost time. To ensure the safety of all concerned, he decided to obtain a towing vessel – the steam yacht *Elphin (Elfin)* from Birkenhead.

At 10pm on the 24th February 1880 they set off again. It quickly became apparent that *Elphin* would have to assume her towing duties because a gale had blown up. Matters soon became quite desperate; off Great Ormes Head they had to transfer the three personnel from the *Resurgam* to *Elphin* to help with towing. Mounting seas swamped the *Resurgam*, and because her conning tower could not be closed from the outside, she began to fill with sea water. Next morning, the 25th February, about 10am, she snapped her towline and sank.

However, the run of disasters had not ended. The *Elfin* ran for shelter in the Dee and anchored off Mostyn. The wind changed, her anchor chains broke, and she was adrift. The *Iron King* came to assist; but rammed the *Elfin* by mistake, sinking her on the Salisbury Middle Bank in the Dee. She was a total loss. Garrett tried to get help in Liverpool to look for the missing vessel, but the February gales continued and nobody was prepared to venture out to what was, after all, a salvage job and not a ship in distress. By great good fortune, nobody was killed.

Later, the search for *Resurgam* began. The problems facing any salvage were numerous. To begin with, she was very tiny – 45ft (15 metres) long – but weighed 30 tons. She could, therefore, be easily "absorbed" into a sandbank. Her heavy build was due to the fact that she was a vessel that had to withstand great internal and external pressures. Add to this the fact that the exact location of her final dive was not known – she may have drifted for miles after her cable parted before sinking. Subsequent press cuttings from *The Daily Post* make intriguing, if conflicting, reading. They are paraphrased for convenience.

1969: 24th April The National Committee for Nautical Archaeology (NCNA) sought two vital pieces of information: precisely when and where did the submarine sink? With this information diving operations could be initiated "to retrieve this piece of nautical history." The North West Area representative was a Dr P.N. Davies, lecturer in Economics at Liverpool University, who opined that, as she was iron-built to withstand pressure, "one would think she would have survived better than many other wrecks."

1969: 5th May The NCNA reported that they had reason to believe that *Resurgam* may have sunk off Rhyl, after breaking away from its moorings – which seems to propose a totally different version of the disaster. They had a further report that, in the 1930s, a Liverpool yachtsman (the late Mr Charles Birchall) "complained of fouling a large cylindrical object at low water near Rhyl." Hopes of discovery were raised and the possibility was projected of *Resurgam* being buried under Mostyn Deep because the latter had shoaled considerably over the previous half-century (i.e. up to 1969).

The mystery remains... or so the writer thought, until he saw in *The Daily Post* for 18th December 1995, then in the *Liverpool Echo* for 8th January 1996, that the missing first steam submarine had been found – by accident! A Chester diver, Mr Keith Hurley, went down to untangle a fishing trawler's nets off Rhyl – and came across the encrusted hull of *Resurgam*. A remarkable and timely coincidence, as far as this book is concerned! (The press photographs seemed to impart to her the look and atmosphere of something from outer space.)

Moves are afoot to raise the missing submarine and put her on display, perhaps alongside the other two historic warships in Birkenhead's East Dock – the submarine *Onyx* and the cruiser *Plymouth* - via the Warships Trust. No doubt other Museums will be making a bid to house this remarkable vessel, so she may be embroiled in more in-fighting than she ever experienced as a submarine. She should be kept on Merseyside, of course, and it will not be difficult to imagine the protective and possessive attitude of Merseysiders. (An excellent reference book, *The Life of Rev George Garrett Pasha, Father of the Submarine* by William Scanlan Murphy, Kimber, London, 1987, contains much fascinating background detail about the inventor. There is a copy in the Maritime Museum Archives Section. Also *The Engineer Magazine* for 1882 contains the drawings accompanying this item)

First Ship's Radio, 1901

1901?: The first ship to be fitted with **Marconi wireless** was the Elder Dempster ship, *Lake Champlain*. (It might be noted that Marconi did not invent radio. See: Inventor of Radio – Sir Oliver Lodge in the Science and Technology section.)

1903: The first ship to establish simultaneous wireless contact with both sides of the Atlantic was the Cunard liner *Lucania*. (D.P., 9th June 1969)

1910: The first person to be arrested via the medium of the ship's wireless was **Dr Crippen.** A famous Liverpool landlady, Ma Egerton, has been credited with giving the Police the vital information that led to the arrest. She had been on the stage in London with Crippen's wife, Belle Elmore, and knew her well. When Belle was reported missing, a police search ensued. About that time, Ma Egerton went to London and chanced to meet Crippen and his new lady, Ethel Le Neve, in a London pub. Ma Egerton recognised a particular piece of jewellery that Le Neve was wearing as being one of Belle Elmore's favourite pieces of jewellery. She became suspicious and informed the police. They went to Crippen's house, but he had fled. A search of the premises led to the discovery of Belle Elmore's murdered body in the cellar. The police hunt began for Crippen and Le Neve.

It transpired that they had sailed on the *Montrose*, bound for Canada, with Ethel Le Neve disguised as a boy. The Captain of the ship was alerted by radio and recognised the two miscreants from the description supplied. They were arrested on board and handed over to the authorities in Halifax, Nova Scotia, pending their return to England for trial and punishment.

1909: It was a Liverpool ship, the Cunard *SS Slavonia*, that sent **the first radio distress signal** (i.e. the first "S.O.S.") when she was wrecked off the Azores on 10th June.

First Sea-Going Radio Officer

In 1957, William Davies, of Winstanley Road, Waterloo, died in Walton Hospital, aged eighty. He was **Radio Officer No.1**, as recorded in the records of Marconi International Marine Communication (MIMC). Starting as a GPO telegraphist, he joined MIMC in 1902 and remained with them until his retirement in 1953. His proud boast was that he had never been on the Marconi sick list during his half century of service with them. He was made an M.B.E. for his services to marine radio.

Institute of Coastal Oceanography and Tides, 1919

This Institute – **the first in the British Empire** – was originally entitled **the Liverpool Tidal Institute** and was established on Bidston Hill in 1919. **It was the first research centre to carry out an intensive study of storm surges and to produce methods (models) for forecasting them.** It was also the **first to study the tilts of the earth caused by tides**. It has been discovered, for instance, that the weight of water at high tide in the Mersey causes the Wirral Peninsula to tip towards the Mersey. The Institute – the big, light-coloured building on Bidston Hill near the old Bidston Lighthouse – is a Department of Liverpool University. (See: Proudman, below.) It is worth recalling that the study of tides and tidal effect has had a long history locally:

¤   Jeremiah Horrox (see Science)

¤   William Hutchinson, who kept **a register of tides from 1768 to 1793**. His observations form the basis of present-day tide tables. (See: William Hutchinson)

¤   William Whewell and Sir John Lubbock, both nationally-known figures, discovered Hutchinson's Tide Tables and used them, in 1830, to develop the **Theory of Tides.**

¤   Joseph Proudman, in 1916, developed **a mathematical theory of the action of tides** at the Department of Oceanography, Liverpool (later linked with Bidston Tidal Institute).

First Passenger Motor Ship, 1920

1920: The Elder Dempster Line had **the first British passenger motor ship, the *Aba*.** (D.P., 22nd May 1969)

Fumigation, 1923

Possibly the greatest curse on board ship is infestation by rats. Apart from the damage they do to cargoes, there is the ever-present danger of disease. They multiply at an alarming rate and are hard to control – especially where there is food available in large quantities. It is a problem that has plagued mariners probably from the very beginning of shipping. In 1923, perhaps the most effective step forward was made in the fight against these pests when **cyanide gas was used for the first time in a ship in the British Isles,** in Liverpool. It was considered such an important breakthrough that the Minister of Health of that time attended – Neville Chamberlain.

PLUTO

The invasion of France (D-Day) depended for its continuing success on great quantities of fuel. To have supplied these by conventional tankers would have been inadequate and highly dangerous (considering the vulnerability of a tanker to dive-bombing). Hence another means was needed for supplying fuel. It was decided by the scientists and War Cabinet that the solution lay in **PLUTO – Pipe Line Under The Ocean**.

The idea was to uncoil a long, flexible pipeline on the bed of the English Channel. After a bridgehead had been established, fuel would be pumped along this pipeline from England to the Normandy beaches. The fuel for this pipeline was to be unloaded at Liverpool, and to enable this to be achieved quickly, and with a rapid flow, a platform was constructed off the east bank of the Mersey, opposite what is now the Britannia pub at the Garden Festival site. A yellow buoy marks the spot today.

The American and English tankers came to this staging, tied up and linked their hoses to hoses on the staging. Fuel was then pumped down the pipes, under the Mersey, down the length of England to emerge at a pumping point on the South Coast – then under the Channel to France. It was a brilliant idea, and it worked well.

Port Radar

The First Radar Controlled Ferry system in the world was installed at Seacombe in 1948. The original scanner can still be seen on top of the Seacombe Ferry tower, and it is still in use, though being updated at the present time (January 1996). Prior to this electronic magic, ferries relied on a tolling bell on each landing-stage to guide them from one stage to the other. To avoid collision, the ferries' own sirens were also used if need be, and booming out over every other sound was the famous "Bootle Bull" – a giant foghorn mounted on the dock wall in Bootle to warn shipping in the foggy conditions. It is now preserved at the Albert Dock.

The first Port Radar in the world was established in **1948** at **the north-west corner of Gladstone Dock**. The original circular tower is still standing. Using this shore-based radar station, all shipping in the river could be monitored and, if necessary, brought safely to an anchorage or dock, even in fog. The first radar set, made by Sperry, was replaced a decade later by a more modern set, **the Decca Type 32**, made by Decca Radar Ltd. (Southampton, London and Hamburg were all eventually fitted with the Decca 32.) A new building was also erected alongside the 26 metres (80ft) tower at Gladstone Dock, at the same time, to house the new electronic equipment. The site had a clear view over 14 miles of buoyed channel out to the Bar Light Vessel, and beyond the Liver Building, up-river, to New Ferry.

The original radio-telephone installation at the station – to enable exchange of radio messages between ships and Radar Control – was supplied by the Automatic Telephone and Electric Company of Liverpool, but the later R/T sets were supplied by Marconi's Wireless Telegraph Company.

The navigational assistance given to ships by the original station included, in bad weather, regular situation reports to ships' pilots by radio, describing the position and/or movement of every ship either at anchor or under way in the river and the Approaches. Weather reports were also supplied. Modern equipment also supplies these services – and more. (For readers requiring more technical information, there is a good article in the magazine *The Shipping World*, February 11th 1959 edition, pages 199 and 200. It is available in the Picton.)

More recently (1987) a new, state-of-the-art, radar system was installed and ultimately commisioned (1993) at the north-west corner of the Royal Seaforth Container Base. It has an unusual shape, aptly described by children on recent ferry trips as "the Giant Cornetto"! It contains very expensive and highly sophisticated electronic equipment, but the remarkable fact is that nobody works there. All signals (i.e. all radar information regarding shipping) are transferred by fibre-optic cable transmission to the Port Operations Control Centre at Seaforth.

The Seaforth unit is one of three important radar focus points for the Mersey and its Approaches. A second radar unit is situated at Point Lynas (Anglesey) which transfers its data by dedicated telephone line to the Seaforth Headquarters, some 80 miles away. The third part of this electronic web of essential information is situated on the Mersey Tunnel Ventilation Shaft Building in Birkenhead (near Woodside Ferry) to give radar coverage of the Eastham and Garston Channels. Data is transferred to Seaforth by fibre optic cable and microwave link.

A visit to the Port Operations Control Centre at Seaforth is like visiting the bridge of the *Starship Enterprise*. There are huge TV consoles (technically, Norcontrol VOC 5000 display consoles with traffic displays, alphanumeric monitors and one Norcontrol VMC 5000 with video recorders and printers). These can display the state of shipping within an 18 mile radius of Point Lynas, and from beyond the Bar Buoy (which replaced the old *Bar Lightship*) to Seaforth and into the Mersey as far as Eastham. The consoles themselves can enlarge or diminish the widest or the most minute of features (i.e. a zoom facility), and when supplemented by audio data, can supply the operators with a vast range of information vital to the safe docking or departure of big and small vessels. Point Lynas supplied 1000 services in 1995, Seaforth supplied 6000. If we think of these numbers in terms of ships assisted, then we can appreciate the volume of shipping entering and leaving this Port.

(After due consideration, it is the writer's opinion that, compared with the Port Operations Control Centre at Seaforth, the bridge of the *Starship Enterprise* comes a poor second!) [Information supplied by Capt. Knuckey and staff at Port Operations, MD & HC, Seaforth.]

Floating Cranes, 1920

A port with the extensive dock system and variety of cargoes that Liverpool once controlled would have had great need of at least one heavy-lift crane. A typical example comes to mind: the shipping of railway steam engines, made in Lancashire, to foreign parts (e.g. India and China, where so many are still in use). The problem was resolved in 1920 when a giant floating crane, the *Mammoth*, was given by Germany as part of their war reparations at the end of World War 1. The crane had a 150 ton lifting capacity and, with its massive steel-framed structure, was an impressive sight on the Mersey skyline. Its sister-ship, the *Samson*, was a similar but smaller craft with a 50 ton lift.

These two floating giants gave sterling service right up to 1986 when they were sold to Holland and were replaced by the new *Mersey Mammoth*. This giant is a very slimmed-down version, but it can lift 250 tons on its main "hook" – known in nautical circles as a "block" – and 50 tons on its smaller, but faster-operating, block. Its delicate-looking jib belies its strength. **It also possesses a unique feature: it is self-propelled with two horizontally mounted screws (propellers).** The screws are not vertical as, for instance, the screws on one of the ferryboats, but lie flat, in a horizontal plane, under the bottom of the ship. They are individually controlled by a large joystick each. By juggling the positions of the two joysticks, this unique ship (for so she is regarded) can progress forwards, backwards or sideways, and can edge into the most awkward quayside anywhere in Britain. **She is the largest floating crane on the West Coast in the UK.**

She may occasionally be seen in other ports, doing various odd jobs of lifting cargoes, new quayside fittings and so on because, like everything else in use in the docks, she has to earn her keep. Her top speed is only seven-and-a-half knots, so she can only cope with strong headwinds by "tacking" from side to side like a sailing ship! One of these odd jobs was to take very large circular "collars" from Cammell-Laird's to the Nuclear Submarine Base at Faslane, where the collars were welded on to the hull of each submarine. One of these trips ended in hilarious fashion.

It had been reported in the press (unfortunately), some years ago, that some of these collars had been welded upside down on to the nuclear submarines, to the acute embarrassment of the Navy! Their embarrassment was even further increased when, on the next trip to Faslane, the *Mersey Mammoth*'s crew, unknown to their skipper, prepared a surprise for the Naval personnel there. As the huge floating crane began to unload the next batch of giant steel collars, a message was seen, painted in large white letters, on the side of each collar. It read, quite simply, "THIS SIDE UP ".

No doubt the Naval apoplexy which erupted was eventually cured by imbibing something stronger than "sippers". ("Sippers" are best explained to the reader by an ex-Naval man.)

First Guided Missile Ship, 1960

Built by Cammell-Laird's for the Royal Navy in 1960, the **first guided missile destroyer** was named *HMS Devonshire* – the eighth ship to bear that name since 1692. She was 520ft (170 metres) overall with a 54ft (18 metres) beam, and weighed 5000 tons. Her armament consisted of one "Seaslug" guided weapons system on the quarter-deck; four radar-controlled 4.5inch guns in twin mountings forrard; two "Seacat" close-range guided weapons fitted abaft the after funnel; a Westland *Wessex* helicopter; and the latest under-water detection equipment. She was the first destroyer to be fitted out as a complete "hunter – killer".

First Computer-Controlled Administration, 1962

The Mersey Docks and Harbour Board became **the first port authority in the UK to be equipped with a computer.** A visit, say, to the MD&HC Marine Division today, would reveal several computers of a highly specialised and electronically sophisticated nature.

First Direct Sailing to Japan

In 1967, the Blue Funnel Line provided **the first ever direct sailing from the UK to Japan.** This was accomplished by the *Maron* which sailed from Birkenhead to Japan via Panama. The trip was occasioned by the closing of the Suez Canal by General Nasser of Egypt. (D.P. 4/8/69)

Hovercraft

For most Merseysiders, **the hovercraft experiment** during 1962 was their first encounter with the maritime future. This new craft (" Aircraft or ship?" was the burning question of the day) was very much in the experimental stage, and the idea of running a regular Hovercraft Mail Service across a major river estuary was a revolutionary one. If the idea was proven to be economically and mechanically successful, it would link places by a short sea route, so replacing long and tedious journeys round coastal inlets and estuaries. As usual, the longest part of the experiment was the time spent obtaining permissions from the GPO (as it was then), Parliament and various local councils.

The Wallasey area was chosen as the start terminus, and the day the experiment team went to examine likely landing places on the North Wales coast, their car was held up for a very long time at what used to be a notorious bottleneck at Queensferry. Many of us have unhappy memories of that particular traffic black spot. This proved to be a most convincing argument for the establishment of a much quicker mode of egress to North Wales – viz. the Hovercraft Service. It's an ill wind!

Hoylake was first choice for a terminus on the Wirral, but the noise of the four powerful jet engines on the *Vickers VA-3* hovercraft caused some heart-flutterings in that pleasant residential area so the team wearily agreed to try again. Eventually they settled for the more open and less populated area of Leasowe shore. Two other craft had been considered – the *Britten – Norman CC2* and the *Denny Sidewall*. The Vickers won the day because its capability of carrying 24 passengers was a more economically viable proposition.

On Friday, 20th July 1962, the first service left Leasowe for Rhyl (ten minutes late due to the interest of the press). It arrived 25 minutes later. **The Rhyl-Wallasey Hovercraft Mail Service was born.** There were four return runs each day, and this 25-minute regular mail service lasted until Sunday, 16th September 1962 – interrupted only by the bad weather for which the area is especially notorious. It had made its point during its three-month trial – major estuaries could be crossed regularly by Hovercraft in safety and relative comfort, and it could be made economically viable. It was modern, it was exciting, and it was a First for the whole country, which was made fully aware of the experiment through the new medium of television.

Royal Seaforth Container Terminal

The **first ship to enter the new Container Terminal** was *Tasmania Star*, a 12,000 ton meat ship. The Terminal handled 100 000 containers in the first year of operation. To construct the container base, some six million cubic metres of clay and soil were dug out. The outer wall is a massive structure built up of huge blocks of rock from Dinmor (Anglesey), Wales, Carnforth, and Parbold,(Lancashire). The Container Terminal is part of Liverpool Freeport.

Liverpool Freeport

The Freeport – the 600 acre "icing on the cake" for the Port – was opened by Her Royal Highness, Princess Anne, in November 1984. It was the **largest of six freeports** created at that time to stimulate trade in areas of special economic difficulty (Southampton, London, Felixstowe, and Manchester and Heathrow Airports were the other five). The idea was to encourage trade by cutting out several levies while ships/aircraft remained in the freeport area. These levies are Value Added Tax (VAT); Import duty; and EEC agricultural levies. Further, if the incoming commodity is processed in some way within the Freeport boundary, then exported to a non-EEC country, the three levies are still not paid.

Liverpool is the most successful Freeport in the UK. This is not surprising when some of the operating aims and procedures are realised:

¤   Container ships (e.g. Atlantic Container Lines) have to lock in, berth, unload, reload and lock out in under eleven-and-a- half hours.

¤   The aim is to have lorries on the dock estate for no more than 40 minutes.

¤   Cargoes are expected to be moved immediately by the owners so that there is no need for storage at the dock.

¤   A cargo of 75,000 tons of grain is unloaded at the rate of 20,000 tons per day – i.e. in three-and-a-half days. In the "good old days" it took three weeks or more.

¤   **Liverpool is the largest exporter of scrap metal in the UK.** The scrap metal is shredded down or "minced" so that individual items take up less space. Hence, much more can be loaded on any one ship.

¤   Thanks to the *Freightliner* service linking Seaforth to Dover and the Chunnel, this "Landbridge" – the only major port linking linking Ireland and the Continent – enables an ACL ship (for instance) to be on its way back to the USA while its previous cargo is en route to mainland Europe.

From the MD&HC's *Factfile* for Spring 1996 comes the following: "**Liverpool is the major UK port for trade with the Eastern Seaboard of North America.** It is also in the top five British container ports."

The Terminal also houses the grain silos belonging to the MD&HC which supply many big outlets, including Kelloggs and Allied Grain. **Liverpool is the leading port in the country for importing grain.** Timber imports at Seaforth make Liverpool **the largest timber port in Great Britain.**

Again, the reader is urged to go on an organised Dock Tour to appreciate the enormous quantities of cargo, the wide selection of handling aids (straddle-carriers, the *Mersey Mammoth*, the giant blue cranes, grain suction pipes, etc.) and the variety of goods shipped.

Containers being unloaded from an ACL ship

The Lifeboat Service

Britain's first Lifeboat Station, and the first in the world, was established at Formby, Lancashire, and opened in 1776. (See: William Hutchinson, 1715-1801)

The Liverpool to Holyhead Semaphore Telegraph

"I'll put a girdle round the earth in forty minutes." (Puck's reply to Oberon in Shakespeare's *Midsummer Night's Dream*.)

The secret of success in the shipping business was (and still is) rapid intelligence. In 1763, strollers on the Liverpool waterfront were often treated to a remarkable display of flag-raising on Bidston Hill. Along the top of the hill, on a north-south axis, were raised over 80 flagpoles, each one allocated to a particular shipowner (some owners had more than one pole). If the lighthouse keeper at Bidston trained his telescope on Point Lynas, Anglesey, and saw a ship or ships rounding that famous Point, he would run outside and raise the house flag(s) of the owner(s) whose ship(s) had been spotted. Runners on the Liverpool waterfront then raced with the news to the Lyceum (bottom of Bold Street), where the shipowners were awaiting such news. Then the bargaining began.

The obvious limitation of this system was visibility. Rain squalls, sea mist

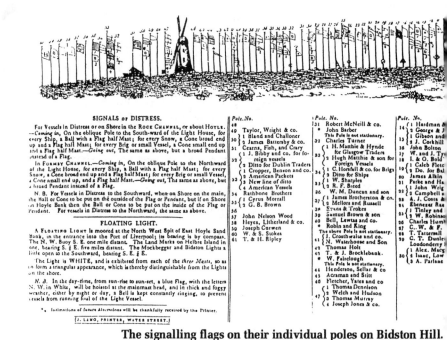

SIGNALS OF DISTRESS.

For Vessels in Distress or on Shore in the ROCK CHANNEL, or about HOYLE. —*Coming* in, On the oblique Pole to the South-ward of the Light House, for every Ship, a Ball with a Flag half Mast; for every Snow, a Cone broad end up and a Flag half Mast; for every Brig or small Vessel, a Cone small end up and a Flag half Mast.—*Going out*, The same as above, but a broad Pendant instead of a Flag.

In FORMBY CHANNEL.—*Coming* in, On the oblique Pole to the Northward of the Light House, for every Ship, a Ball with a Flag half Mast; for every Snow, a Cone broad end up and a Flag half Mast; for every Brig or small Vessel, a Cone small end up, and a Flag half Mast.—*Going out*, The same as above, but a broad Pendant instead of a Flag.

N. B. For Vessel in Distress to the Southward, when on Shore on the main, the Ball or Cone to be put on the outside of the Flag or Pendant, but if on Shore on Hoyle Bank then the Ball or Cone to be put on the inside of the Flag or Pendant. For vessels in Distress to the Northward, the same as above.

FLOATING LIGHT.

A FLOATING LIGHT is moored at the North West Spit of East Hoyle Sand Bank, in the entrance into the Port of Liverpool; its bearing is by compass, The N. W. Buoy S. E. one mile distant. The Land Marks on Helbre Island in one, bearing S. ¼ E. five miles distant. The Mockbeggar and Bidston Lights a little open to the Southward, bearing S. E. ¼ E.

The Light is WHITE, and is exhibited from each of the *three Masts*, so as to form a triangular appearance, which is thereby distinguishable from the Lights on the shore.

N. B. In the day-time, from sun-rise to sun-set, a blue Flag, with the letters N. W. in White, will be hoisted at the mainmast head, and in thick and foggy weather, either by night or day, a Bell is kept constantly ringing, to prevent vessels from running foul of the Light Vessel.

. Intimations of future Alterations will be thankfully received by the Printer.

[J. LANG, PRINTER, WATER STREET.]

Pole. No.		Pole. No.		Pole. No.	
48	Taylor, Wright & co.	31	Robert McNeill & co.	14	1 Hardman &
49	1 Bland and Challoner	*	John Barber This Pole is not stationary.		2 George & J
50	2 James Battersby & co.	32	Charles Turner	15	1 Gibson and 2 J. Corkhill
51	Cearns, Fish, and Crary		1 H. Mathie & Hynde for Glasgow Traders	16	John Bolton
52	1 J. Bibby and co. for foreign vessels	33	2 Hugh Matthie & son for Foreign Vessels	17	W. and J. T
	2 Ditto for Dublin Traders		1 C. Horsfall & co. for Brigs	18	I. & O. Bold
53	1 Cropper, Benson and co.	34	2 Ditto for Ships	19	1 Caleb Flet 2 Do. for Bal
	2 American Packets	35	1 W. Sharples	20	James Alkin
	3 New line of ditto		2 R. F. Breed	21	Parke and Ha
	4 American Vessels	36	W. M. Duncan and son	22	1 John Wrig
54	Rathbone Brothers	37	1 James Brotherston & co.		2 Campbell s
55	1 Cyrus Morrall		2 Mellors and Russell	23	A. J. Costa &
	2 G. B. Brown	38	Evans & Frokes	24	Ebenezer Ras
56		39	Samuel Brown & son	25	1 Tinley and
57	John Nelson Wood	40	Bell, Lewtas and co.		2 W. Robinson
58	Heyes, Litherland & co.		Robin and King This Pole is not stationary.	26	Charles Hurst
59	Joseph Carwen	41	1 Croathwaite and co.	27	C. W. & F.
60	W. & S. Stokes		2 N. Waterhouse and Son	28	T. Tattersall
61	T. & H. Ripley	42	Thomas Holt	29	C. T. Dunlo Londonderry
		43	T. & J. Brocklebank.	30	1 Alex. Macg
		*	W. Fairclough This Pole is not stationary.		2 Isaac, Low
		44	Henderson, Sellar & co		3 A. Parlane
		45	Acraman and Stitt		
		46	Fletcher, Yates and co		
		47	1 Thomas Dennison		
			2 Welch and Hudson		
			3 Thomas Murray		
			4 Joseph Jones & co.		

The signalling flags on their individual poles on Bidston Hill.

or fog prevented the sightings being made. After trying one or two flag-signalling systems (from ship to shore, and vice versa), the Dock Trustees realised that a more reliable system was needed. They petitioned Parliament and an Act was passed in June 1925 "for the further improvement of the Port, Harbour and Town of Liverpool." The Dock Trustees were thereby empowered to: "establish a speedy Mode of Communication to the Shipowners and Merchants at Liverpool of the arrival of Ships and Vessels off the Port of Liverpool or the Coast of Wales, by building, erecting and maintaining Signal Houses, Telegraphs or such other Modes of Communication as to them shall seem expedient, between Liverpool and Hoylake, or between Liverpool and the Isle of Anglesey."

This Act not only reflected Liverpool's needs, but also the South's awareness of the value to London pockets of Liverpool's maritime successes, innovations and increasing trade.

A line of eleven signalling stations was built. Each station had a building with the signalling apparatus outside. The latter consisted of a tall mast

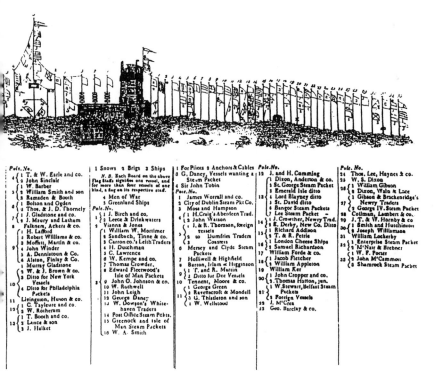

(from Holden's Liverpool Almanac and Tide Table)

THE ORIGINAL TELEGRAPH STATIONS

The names and positions of the original stations are here listed, the distances(in nautical miles) being those between each station.

HOLYHEAD	At the West end of Holy Island on Holyhead Mountain about 500ft, between the North and South Stacks	Start
CHURCH BAY	At Gareglwyd (Anglesea), known as Mount Pleasant, near to the village of Llanfaethlu	6.2 miles
LLANEILIAN (Anglesey)	Sometimes known as Paris Mountain [more correctly, Parys Mountain]. At 300 ft, overlooking Point Lynas which was the cruising ground of the Mersey pilots, and called the "Dungeness of the North"	10.8 miles
PUFFIN ISLAND	(Ynys Seiriol), also known as Priestholm	13.0 miles
GREAT ORME	Llandudno. Station at summit, at 670 ft [Fig. 72].	7.0 miles
LLYSFAEN	Behind Old Colwyn, at 670 ft [Fig. 71].	8.7 miles
FORYD	On the beach at the West end of Rhyl	6.7 miles
GOLDEN GROVE	Site inland from Prestatyn, at 770 ft	6.0 miles
HILBRE ISLAND	At the mouth of the Dee, at sea level	7.2 miles
BIDSTON HILL	Next to Bidston lighthouse.. Prominently in view from the Pier Head, Liverpool	6.4 miles
LIVERPOOL	Watchman on permanent daylight watch from Tower Building/ St. Nicholas' Church/Duncan's Warehouse	3.5 miles

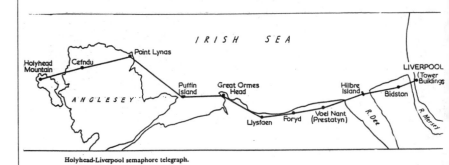

Holyhead-Liverpool semaphore telegraph.

The original semaphore telegraph system

(Baltic pine), about 15 metres (40 to 50ft) tall and 55 centimetres (22 inches) in diameter, with a top-mast above cross-trees. The mast included oak "fishes" – added tapered lengths of timber, for strength – bound round it and held with iron hoops. The actual semaphore arms were made of African oak, six feet long, and operated by ropes and pulleys. The whole structure was built to withstand the full force of westerlies as well as the operation of the signal arms and ropes by (no doubt enthusiastic) amateurs.

The system was undoubtedly fast. The record for sending a signal from Holyhead, via all the stations, to Liverpool was eight minutes! Admittedly, it was a three-figure code signal, but the signal arms had to be hoisted up and down by ropes and pulleys.

The writer was participating in research into this telegraph system at Liverpool University in 1993/4, when the Liverpool signal station was discovered by Mr Frank Large on the famous Ackermann Print. The reader is invited to share in the thrill of rediscovering the Liverpool Station – Duncan's Warehouse, off Chapel Street – by applying a good magnifying glass to the illustration below and looking for the crossed signal arms which can be seen about 2.5 cm to the left of the base of St Nicholas's spire.

Part of the Ackerman print revealing the end of the semaphore line in Liverpool

The cost of erecting the station houses, masts and arms (£1700) was reasonable (even if brought up to today's value by multiplying by 150) when weighed against the enormous value of the cargoes being protected and the immense profits accruing from early intelligence.

Mistakes were made, and were very sharply dealt with! The following tart letter, from the Marine Surveyor, Mr I. Roberts, to Hugh Evans, in charge of the Holyhead Signal Station, illustrates the point:

```
"Sir,

Number 2163, Helena, brigantine, was reported yesterday
instead of No.2153, Heart of Oak (which number started
correct from Holyhead) from Mauritius belonging to Messrs
Gladstone and Co, which vessel was anxiously expected. The
signals are forwarded in a very careless manner and
unusually slow.

Yr. obedient servant,

I. Roberts."
```

Details of the signal stations are added in the accompanying figure. The whole line was a very lucrative First for Liverpool.

SPORT

Horse Racing

The greatest horse race in the world is undoubtedly the Grand National, run at Aintree every Spring. It was introduced as a Steeplechase at Maghull (near Aintree) by Lord "Dashalong" Sefton in 1837, then two years later it was transferred to Aintree, with its title changed to Liverpool Grand Steeple Chase. It was handicapped in 1843 and became the **Grand National Steeplechase**. In recent years there have been two last-minute problems: in 1993 a broken starting tape led to a disastrous start, which resulted in the race being cancelled; in 1997, the 150th Grand National was postponed until the following Monday because of a bomb scare.

For the writer's generation it still holds many memories. There was the annual Jump Sunday (the Sunday before the National) when the public were admitted to the course to walk round and "weigh up" (in Lancashire parlance) the jumps. There were stalls of all kinds supplying food or racing information and thousands of cloth-capped men inspecting everything with a judicious eye – the height of the jumps, the horses, the jockeys, the owners, the going – before deciding on the Winner of their choice. "Hope springs eternal in the human breast," indeed! Finally, for the inexpert, there was the famous Prince Monolulu who would attract the crowd with his famous shout of "I've gorra n'orse" – meaning the name of the winner – then would share this top secret information with anyone who was prepared to invest at an agreed premium. The claim that he named every horse in the National was never substantiated, but "you can't be hanged for what you're thinking" was one lady's assertion!

For the writer's money (to continue in the parlance of the race-course), the greatest First at Aintree was the record set up by **Red Rum in winning the National three times and coming second twice.** He also won the Scottish Grand National. No horse was ever greeted with the adulation and affection Red Rum received, even being deeply mourned when he died (1995) and being buried in front of the Main Stand, just by the Winning Post which he had passed so often and so successfully at Aintree. His training included long gallops on the sands at Southport and Ainsdale. (The writer reserves the right to shed an unashamed tear or two, for he was at Aintree for every race Red Rum won – to the writer's financial advantage!)

The first, and probably the last, man to go jumping round the National Course without a horse was Tom Scott, father of a Mayor of Bootle. In 1870, Scott, who was a well-known athlete, jumped over every jump on the Aintree Course. The only concession he was allowed was to jump the Water Jump in the reverse direction to that normally taken by the field. (D.P., 3rd April 1969.)

The Derby, run at Epsom, owed its foundation to Lord Derby in 1780, but it is not generally known that the race originated in flat-racing on Leasowe Sands, near Leasowe Castle (North Wirral) in the 18th century. There was horse-racing on the flat, in the Aintree area, in Queen Elizabeth I's time.

Boxing

One of Britain's greatest boxing champions was John Conteh, from Northwood, Kirkby. He was British, Commonwealth, and European Light Heavyweight Champion, before **going on to win the World title in 1974.** He was the first Briton to do this since 1930. The **first female Boxing Coach in Europe** is Sharon Willis, who trained at the Rotunda Club in Kirkdale. (*Liverpool Echo*, 19th March 1994)

Cricket

In 1868, **Bootle C.C., played the Australian Cricket XI.** They played two games against this Australian Touring XI (a team of Aboriginals), thus stealing a lead over other Merseyside Clubs. (Reg Brookes in the *Daily Post*, 9th May 1968.) The Australians stole a lead over Bootle by hammering them by nine wickets in the first game and by 154 runs in the second game. The game was played at the old Irlam Road Ground.

Bootle's status was such that, in 1865, they could arrange a fixture with an All-England side (Bootle beaten!), then some years later, against a South of England Team (which included W.G. Grace). The Bootle Team were allowed to field 22 players – and won!

Ian Botham, the famous all-rounder, who played for England with great distinction, was born in Heswall, Wirral.

Cycling

1867: Liverpool Velocipedes established Britain's, and perhaps the world's, **first cycling club.**

Football

There is only one real religion in Liverpool – football – with places of worship at Goodison Park and Anfield to witness the claim. Any self-respecting Liverpudlian worthy of the name will have learnt the histories of these two great Football Clubs in his/her cradle, so there is no need for these to be recounted here. However, the same self-respecting Liverpudlian would never forgive the omission of the Firsts created by Everton (The Blues) and Liverpool (The Reds) since their foundation.

Everton were the first Club (in the 60s) to install **under-soil heating** to allow games to be played in frosty weather. Under-soil heating was invented by Liverpool City Electrical Engineer, Percival James Robinson. They were also **the first to build a dug-out** at the side of the pitch (near the Players' entrance).

"Give it to Dixie!" This famous Goodison Park battle cry used to ring out round the ground in the late 20s and 30s when the world-famous centre-forward, Ralph (Dixie) Dean, was playing for Everton. He was a phenomenal goal-scorer, especially with his head. He was **the first to score 60 goals in one season,** in 1927/28 and set **a still-unbeaten record of 82 goals in one season**. The writer, as a somewhat mystified 4-year-old, was taken to Goodison by his father to see the latter achievement. The chief memory is of a man going round the ground ringing a bell when Dixie scored.

Liverpool F.C. has seen great glory and terrible tragedy since the days of "Shankly's Red Army". The Hillsborough disaster left a terrible scar on the Liverpool football scene, and traumas are still affecting the lives of relatives and fans who saw 95 adults and children crushed to death on that terrible day. Perhaps the glories of the last 20 years or so may help to assuage the grief of Hillsborough – though it will never eradicate it. Here, then, are some of the Firsts created by The Reds.

1914: The **first "Royal" Cup Final** was played at Crystal Palace between Liverpool and Burnley. Burnley won, 1 – 0.

1965: Liverpool were the first team to be televised in *Match of the Day.*

1969: Liverpool were **the first team to be televised in colour.**

In the late 1920s, at the start of a Derby Game between Everton and Liverpool, **both teams came out on to the pitch together,** for the start of the game, for the first time in the history of football. This idea had been suggested by the late "Bee" Edwards, Sports Editor of the Liverpool Echo, who thought that the practice would encourage a more sporting atmosphere. The idea was later adopted by the Football Association for the Wembley Cup Final.

Goal Nets: John Alexander Brodie, Liverpool City Engineer, **invented football goal nets** in 1892. They were first used at Bolton Wanderer's ground.

Golf

There are 34 golf courses on Merseyside. Whether this constitutes a First or not has yet to be verified. Perhaps someone with a mathematical turn of mind could produce a maths calculation based on the number of Golf Courses per unit of area.

The Amateur Golf Championship was initiated in 1885, by the Royal Liverpool G.C. at Hoylake (Wirral). The Centenary Championship was held at Hoylake in 1995.

1907: A strange wager was made by John Ball - namely, **to go round the Hoylake Course, in dense fog, in under 90 strokes, in less than two-and-a-half hours, and without losing the ball – which was to be black**! He completed the wagered round in 81 minutes – with the same ball! Some of us have been known to take that length of time searching for lost balls in one round!

1937: The **first golf trolley was invented** and used by Frank T. Copnall, a portrait painter, at the Royal Liverpool G.C. at Hoylake, who trundled the first golf trolley along on its pram wheels – or was it cycle wheels? Nobody can remember! Mass-produced trolleys appeared after WW2.

Motorcycling

Geoff Duke, the "flying baker's son" was a St Helens lad. He **won six Motorcycle Championships and five Isle of Man TT Races during the 1950s.**

Rugby

The oldest, though not the first, **Rugby Club in the world** is Liverpool Rugby Club, which was founded in 1857.

Sailing

The International Yacht Racing Union (IYRU) held the **World Team Racing Championship** on the Marine Lake, West Kirby, from 22nd to 26th August 1995. The same site was chosen in 1994 for the **World Windsurfing Championship.**

Snooker

Liverpool claims to have the only **Snooker Museum in the world**, situated in Clare's, the snooker and outdoor games specialists in St Anne Street. The Museum was the lifelong work of Mr Clare, who spent considerable time (and money) researching the game's history. Amongst a host of odd items the Museum contains a scoring board which automatically turned the gas lights off over the snooker table when the score reached 100; a special device for assisting a one-armed man to play; original snooker "cues" as used by Cavalry Officers on the North West Frontier of India, where the game and snooker cues were invented; and an eight-sided table among other things. It is claimed that the game was invented by (Sir) Neville Chamberlain, as a variation of a game called Black Pool, when he was a subaltern with the Devonshire Regiment at Jubbulpore, India, in 1875. He drew up the first rules of Snooker.

Allerton's John Parrott became one of the most popular **world snooker champions** when he defeated Jimmy White in 1991.

Swimming

The first Liverpool woman to swim the English Channel was Catherine Smith, aged 21, of Allerton, on 30th July 1994. The swim lasted 19 hours and had to continue through a thunderstorm off the French coast. She was a member of the **first relay team to swim Loch Ness, both ways,** in a record time of 26hours 13 minutes.

It is claimed that Guinea Gap Baths, on the bank of the Mersey at Wallasey, has **staged more World Championship swims than any other baths in the world.** This could well be true because the Olympic and the World Championships tend to be held at different venues on each occasion, but Guinea Gap was the only venue for years.

All-Rounder par excellence

Charlotte (Lottie) Dod, from Bebington, was one of the world's greatest sports all-rounders. She:

¤　**won the Wimbledon Ladies Championship in 1887, 1888, 1891, 1892 and 1893;**

¤　**won the British Ladies Golf Championship in 1904;**

¤　**won an Olympic Silver for Archery in 1908;**

¤　and played hockey for England.

Presumably, she would have been considered a First lady on all these occasions.

Kirkby Sports Centre

This centre was chosen by the Olympic Committee to host the first **Special Olympic British Games** in 1982.

Youth Hostelling

This "sport for all" entered the ranks of national pastimes in 1929 in Liverpool. It was started by the **Liverpool Ramblers Association** who quickly set up the Merseyside Youth Hostels Association, then set about obtaining hostels. There were six in North Wales and one on the Wirral. The first purpose-built Youth Hostel in Britain was at Maeshafn (near Loggerheads) opened on 26th June 1931. The National Youth Hostels Association came into being in 1930, several months after Merseyside had initiated the movement. (D.P., 15th July 1969.)

TRANSPORT

RAILWAYS

Trade between Liverpool and Manchester, in the early 1800s, was hindered by the lack of a reliable and quick transport system. As a result of the great deposit of debris from retreating glaciers, some 14,000 years ago, south / south-west Lancashire and north Cheshire became covered by large areas of moss and bog, thus hindering the development of transport and any kind of economically useful hinterland. For example, the only effective way of transporting cotton from Liverpool Docks to Manchester was via the River Mersey. Widening of the Mersey above Runcorn had been undertaken in the mid-1700s, and a marked increase in trade between the two towns had resulted. However, advances in shipping and the demands of the cotton industry were creating an urgent need for more rapid means of transport of bulk cargoes, for import and export.

The turnpike roads (1725) had been some help, but not enough to provide the increasing quantities of materials required by this expanding economy. The scientific and technological advances of the time had improved methods of cotton production (the Spinning Jenny, Compton's Mule, etc.), and coal

The 'Rocket', 1829

output from the Lancashire mines was increasingly needed for the cotton mills (winding engines), the iron works (furnaces) and the chemical factories of the Widnes-Warrington area. The eventual arrival of the first railways resulted from the demands of the newest market for coal – viz., steamships.

The idea of a railway was first promoted by Liverpool businessmen around 1822 and a route was surveyed in 1824. A bill was prepared for Parliament but was rejected. A second bill was successful, and the Liverpool and Manchester Railway was conceived – 5th May 1826. Work began in 1827. The Rainhill Trials were run in 1829, from which *Rocket* emerged the winner. The Trials were watched by a young poet who wrote of "the ringing grooves of change" because he thought the trains ran in grooves in the ground. His name? Alfred (Lord) Tennyson.

On 15th September 1830, a new era was born when **the first passenger railway in the world was opened between Liverpool and Manchester**. When these early trains arrived at Edge Hill, Liverpool, the engines were detached from their carriages in the Grand Area at Edge Hill, then the carriages were hauled uphill by wire rope to Crown Street Station by means of a winding engine. After disembarking passengers, then re-loading, the carriages were lowered down to the Grand Area and reunited with their engine. Crown Street Station was **the first train shed** and possessed the first of the **great wooden station roofs**.

In 1836, Lime Street Station was opened. It was **the first station to have iron arcades and to be covered with an overall roof covering the tracks**. Carriages had to be lowered down from Edge Hill Station, via a wire rope, to Lime Street, disembarked and refilled with passengers, then hauled back up to Edge Hill to be reunited with their engine for the journey eastwards. This state of affairs existed until 1890 when the first steam locomotive was built that was strong enough to pull a full "rake" of loaded coaches up the slope, through the tunnels, to Edge Hill.

To relate any more of this fascinating story would require a book in itself, and many excellent ones have been written on the subject. One incident, however, is worth recalling – the death of the MP for Liverpool, William Huskisson, whose legs were badly injured (one being severed) when he was run over by the *Rocket*, at Parkside Station. He died of his injuries that evening – **the first man in the world to be killed by a railway passenger steam engine train**. His biography was later written by a grandson of the man who invented the first through railway-brake; and the irony is that Huskisson would have been saved by that very type of brake had it been invented in his time.

1830: The Post Office first sent letters by rail in 1830 – on the Liverpool and Manchester Railway. (D.P., 26th March 1969)

1838: The first travelling Post Office took the form of a horse box fitted out temporarily as a sorting carriage, and first ran between Liverpool and Birmingham on 6th January 1838 (*Railway Magazine*, December 1994(?), page 649.)

Railway Coupling

Henry Booth (1789-1869) **invented the railway coupling**. He was a corn merchant and a founder and Director of the Liverpool and Manchester Railway Co. He lived at 34 Rodney Street, and a statue of him, in St George's Hall, depicts him holding the railway coupling he invented.

The Mersey Railway

This was **the first underwater railway in the world** – opened in 1886. It achieved two more Firsts: **the first railway in UK to convert from steam to electric power (1903), and the first to introduce the multiple unit system (1903).** In this system, each coach was powered independently of the others. The pumphouse and office block can still be seen at the Pier Head, opposite the Mersey Road Tunnel (Queensway) Ventilator. This railway is still in use as part of Mersey-Rail.

The first Dry Core Cable was laid through the Mersey Railway Tunnel in 1891. (Ref: David Robinson of *Technology Response*.) "Dry core" implied an electric power cable.

On 10th July 1992, a Press Release was issued by Merseyrail informing the public of another First for the Mersey Railway – namely, the addition of **a giant 45-metre-long concrete mural**, entitled *Dream Passage*, at James Street Station on the wall opposite the Wirral bound platform. It depicts images of Liverpool's unique culture and architecture in an original style, and it is **the largest work of art ever to appear in a British railway station.** The £50,000 project was funded by Merseytravel.

Overhead Railway, 1893 to 1956

1888: Work began on the construction of the Liverpool Overhead Railway.

1893: Liverpool Overhead Railway opened. It was the first railway that "ran in the sky" in the provinces. (The City and South London Railway opened on 18/12/1890). It was also **the first elevated electric railway in the world with automatic electric signalling (1893).**

1901: The first railway station escalator in the UK was installed on the

Overhead at Seaforth Sands Station. Ten years later, at London's Earls Court Station, the capital's first railway escalator was installed.

1919: Its peak year, when 18 million passengers were carried. (D.P., 7th Feb. 1969)

1921: First daytime use of coloured light signalling on a permanent basis in UK. (D.P., 8th April 1969)

The railway's working height above the dock Road was 16 feet at its maximum, and there was one place along its length where it descended to road level. This was at the point, just beyond Huskisson Dock (travelling towards Liverpool), where the Lancashire and Yorkshire Company (known to railwaymen as the "L & Y") had constructed a high level line – the Bramley Moore High Level Coal Railway – to supply coal to Bramley Moore Dock for the great ocean liners. Two railways at the same height at the same spot obviously cannot be accommodated so the LOR had to dive down under the L & Y line. This feature was known locally as the Switchback because **the line dived down at a gradient of 1 in 30** (known as the Dive Under), **then rose up at the same gradient on the other side.**

The engineers who designed the structure were Sir Douglas Fox and J.H. Greathead. The contractor was Mr Willans. The Company was promoted under the leadership of Sir William Forwood (his statue is in St John's Gardens). The rail cars ran in groups of three, like the American model, and **were unique in having independent drive on each axle.** One of the cars is maintained today in the Transport Museum, Liverpool Museum, William Brown Street.

A trip along the line from Seaforth to Dingle was a wonderful sight – and a bone-shaking experience! It was better than a school Geography book in the knowledge gained of cargoes, ships, foreign places, and the various scientific advances that had made the line possible. As one sped along at high level, one saw a whole nautical catalogue of famous shipping lines: Cunard, Ellerman, Brocklebank, Furness-Withy, Blue Funnel, Alfred Holt, Harrison, and others.

The stations, from Seaforth to Dingle (a 6.5 mile run) were: Seaforth Sands, Gladstone, Alexandra, Brocklebank, Canada, Huskisson, Nelson, Clarence, Princes, Pier Head, James St., Canning, Wapping, Brunswick, Toxteth, Herculaneum and Dingle.

Its closure, in 1956, was claimed to be unavoidable because of the intensive corrosive action on the metal trackbed due to the action of acid. This had formed when the smoke of the old Dock engines (as they puffed along underneath the Overhead) mixed with rainwater. It would have taken at least two million pounds to refurbish safely. Today, we would have undertaken such a cost quite happily, so great would have been the value of the line as a tourist attraction.

The old Overhead (better known as "the Dockers' Umbrella") is still, today, probably the most mourned loss in the city of Liverpool. Its stanchions can still be seen alongside Wapping Warehouse (on the Dock Road), and its terminus station at Dingle still exists.

ROAD TRANSPORT

Road Haulage

The first successful road haulage operation in the UK is claimed for 1902 when the Road Carrying Company was formed by E. Sharpnell Smith to carry cotton and other bulk cargoes from Liverpool Docks to manufacturing areas in Lancashire. The vehicles involved belonged to Coulthard and Co., and the Lancashire Steam Motor Co. They were 4-ton, 25 hp, steam wagons – 17ft 6 ins (5.5 metres) long and pulling a 2-ton trailer. The business began with nightly runs from Liverpool to Blackburn, in August 1902. A six-ton load took 12 hours for a 40 mile journey. Freight rates varied from 2.5 pence to 6 pence per ton mile. The drivers were paid 33 shillings per week (£1..13s..0d). A London bus driver, at the time, was paid about 25 shillings per week. By the end of the first year, 59 varieties of freight were being moved – from cotton to pickles.

Street Refuges

Crossing a road or a street has been a hazardous business from time immemorial – whether due to the danger of being run down by galloping horses or a Roman chariot or early carriages /stage coaches or the first bikes and cars. Somewhere, there must be records of such occurrences in the past. Today, we have well-documented evidence in the form of road accident returns, and the picture that emerges is one of dreadful increases in injuries and deaths due to a phenomenal increase in road traffic, bad driving, careless pedestrians, etc.

To counteract the problem today, traffic lights control busy junctions, police patrol roads and motorways and speed cameras have been installed at major sets of traffic lights. The needs of pedestrians are also recognised in the creation of Crossing Safety campaigns, the provision of over-passes or under-passes, and the provision of Zebra / Pelican Crossings and safety refuges in the middle of a highway.

Liverpool was first in trying to improve the safety of those crossing roads. **Britain's first recorded street island-refuge for pedestrians was established in 1862** by John Hastings, a saddler by profession, in Lord Street. He was motivated by the death of a prominent stationer, John Walmsley, who was killed while trying to cross that busy road. By the end of 1862 there were six traffic islands which were lit by twin lamp-posts (one at each end of each island) for ensuring safe crossing at night.

Steamrollers

The *sine qua non* of road traffic must surely be the steamroller. It was not invented in Liverpool. but **Liverpool City Council was the first to purchase a steamroller in Britain in 1867.**

Flying Junctions

Motorway junctions are so designed that traffic can filter into or out of a motorway without any severe turning problems or undue reduction of speed. We refer to them familiarly as slip roads. Within Liverpool, junctions at flyovers such as those at Walton (Queens Drive over Rice Lane), or at the Rocket (Queens Drive over M62 etc.) are very convenient to use, yet we owe the idea of such junctions to the early railways.

In 1870, the builders of the Liverpool to Crewe railway (the London and North Western Rly. Co., 1846 to 1923) had the problem of separating the trains going to Liverpool from those going to Glasgow (subsequently the LMS line), without losing time. The solution was **a flying junction at Weaver Junction**, near the River Weaver in Cheshire, which freed the Glasgow trains from the Liverpool line and **allowed an easy change of direction without slowing or stopping**.

Traffic Lights

The first electro-automatic, vehicle-operated traffic signals were made at the **Strowger Works, Edge Lane, Liverpool, in 1932.** They were installed at the corner of Gracechurch St. and Cornhill, London, and were the **first pad-operated ones in Europe**.

First Electric Battery-Driven Bus, 1894

The first experiments in battery-driven trams began in London and a few other places in the 1880s, and they appeared to have a bright future. There had been much discussion as to whether buses should carry their own power

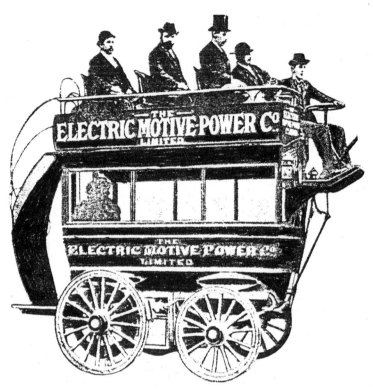

Battery-powered bus, which probably ran on Smithdown Road in 1824

supply (batteries) or be fed from a stationary source (a power generator supplying current along a pick-up rail or wire). A few accumulator trams were tried out in the London area, but did not survive long. A few successes were recorded in the Plaistow and Canning Town area, one of the more successful being the 52-seat, four-wheel double deck cars used by the General Electric Power and Traction Company from 1889 to 1892. A similar car was tried in Liverpool in 1890.

A battery-powered bus appeared briefly on the Smithdown Road route. The only evidence for this appeared in the French magazine, *La Locomotion Terrestre* where there was an illustration with the caption, "L'omnibus electrique de Liverpool." The bus in the illustration showed what is termed "a garden-seat horse bus" converted to battery power, and bearing the title *The Electric Motive Power Co. Limited*. The company was formed in 1884, and was **possibly the first example of a powered bus**.

(Ref: *History of Liverpool Transport – Volume 1*, J.B. Horne and T.B. Maund. Publ: The Light Railway Transport League, Hanwell, Middlesex.)

Trams

The first attempt at establishing a tramway was along the dock road on the Liverpool side of the Mersey in 1859. The MD&HB allowed a Mr W.J. Curtis to operate horse-drawn omnibuses along the railway lines already existing on the dock road. The operators had to pay the Dock Board one shilling for each double journey. Sadly, the charge was too prohibitive, and by February 1860, the service had been withdrawn. The American tramway pioneer, George Francis Train, offered to revive the service, but his offer was not accepted. As it was a specialist railway, it could not be considered a First for the introduction of Trams.

The first "street railway" was proposed by W.& D. Bushy in 1860. In the same year, George Francis Train asked permission from Liverpool Corporation to include West Derby in his list of places to be served. The Corporation were slow to implement Bushys' and Train's recommendations, so the Bushys went ahead and laid the **first track between Fairfield and Old Swan** – about one-and-a-half miles long.

A twelve-inch-wide strip, on each side of the track, was paved with Penmaenmawr granite, the maintainance of which was to be the responsibility of the trustees (The Liverpool Road and Rail Omnibus Company). The opening on 2nd July 1861 was described by the *Daily Post* for 4th July 1861. It stressed the expensive fittings and decoration within the omnibus, including mahogany side panels inlaid with walnut. 40 passengers could be carried (inside and on the roof). Sadly, bad construction, inconvenience to other road users, and much self-doubt about the viability of the scheme led to its removal in 1862 on the orders of the Trustees. Local carters, for instance, had complained of the tram tracks cutting their horses' hooves or wrecking their carts. There is no evidence that these claims were proven.

Meanwhile, Train had written to the Mayor of Liverpool asking for permission to construct and operate trams from the Town Hall to the following disrticts:

- ¤ Aigburth and Garston
- ¤ Kirkdale and Walton
- ¤ Cabbage Hall (near Stanley Park)
- ¤ West Derby
- ¤ Fairfield and Old Swan
- ¤ Edge Hill, Wavertree and Woolton
- ¤ Bootle and Waterloo
- ¤ Rodney Street and Falkner Square
- ¤ Mill Street (south end of Liverpool)

Though the Borough Engineer, James Newlands, was in favour of the scheme in principle, the whole business petered out, so Train turned his attention to the Wirral.

Train's plans were completed and gained for Birkenhead the honour of possessing **the first trams (horse-drawn) in Europe**, in 1861. Records refer to the enthusiasm of the conductor and tram crews in vying with each other at Christmas time by brightening-up their trams with coloured paper-chains! The last Birkenhead tram was withdrawn in 1937. Currently (March 1996), plans are well advanced for the return of a small length of tram-track at Woodside, behind the Ferry, to be equipped with old trams as a heritage feature.

Liverpool eventually produced plans for its own tram service, and was **the first to obtain an Act of Parliament authorising a local tramway service in 1868**. (Two other tramways existed, one in Portsmouth and one on the Isle of Wight, but they were, again, specialist tramways that served boat passengers only.)

Building tram tracks in the middle of the road, within a central reservation, was the brainchild of John A. Brodie (Liverpool's City Engineer). **The first such track in Britain was from Edge Lane to Broadgreen Station, in 1914.** It was extended to Bowring Park the following year. Liverpool stayed ahead of the field as regards central reservations, having nearly a third of its 97 miles of track on reservations. It was appropriate that the last tram to operate in Liverpool was on the Bowring Park route, No 6A – 14th September 1957. John Brodie is commemorated in Brodie Avenue, Mossley Hill.

John Brodie was famous for a much more important reason than central reservations! (See: Sport)

(For an excellent summary of the advent of trams to Liverpool, see *Transactions of the Historic Society of Lancashire and Cheshire* (THSLC), Vol 119, 1967.)

Hydrolastic Suspension

In 1848, the Liverpool Economic Conveyance Co., announced a new type of omnibus with eight wheels: "the whole of which are connected by bars from the axles which give uniform motion to the whole, no wheel being capable of moving without giving a corresponding motion to the other seven". This foreshadowed the later introduction of hydrolastic suspension. (D.P., 4th July 1969)

Motor Charabancs

"Going on the charrer" used to be as important in the Liverpool social calendar as going to the match, or fish on Friday. The accompanying picture (a photograph kindly supplied by Mr A.D. Power) seems to exude the atmosphere special to this great occasion as it depicts a typical "charrer" trip (after the turn of the century) ready to start.

Britain's **first motor charabanc trip** was organised by the late Mr J. Graham Reece, Chairman of the Liverpool automobile firm of Blake & Co., in 1906. The tale was related in the *Daily Post* in its issue for 19th February 1969, as follows: ". . . eighteen members of the Liverpool Club set out for a Sunday ride to Llangollen. The coach's engine was under the passengers' seats, so every time it broke down they had to get out . . . and soon after midnight they had to push the charabanc into a field near Mollington and walk back to Chester to catch a train home! "

Perhaps another First can be claimed for Liverpool, through the good services of Mr Reece, because **he ran the first motor, mail-passenger service in Ireland**, between Ballina and Belmullet. It was very much resented by some of the local residents who vented their indignation by digging a deep trench across the road. "This might have had serious results," commented Mr Reece, "I was glad to be relieved of the contract!" (D.P., as above). Apart from his success with charabancs, Mr Reece, as a leading Liverpool motor trader, was **the first to attach a commercial body (i.e. a van body) to a Ford chassis.** Photographs of this idea appeared in the in-house magazine, *Ford Times*, in the USA. Fords then took up the idea of producing a light van. (D.P., 24th July 1969.)

A 'chara' ready for the day's trip

Buses

If there is one vehicle Liverpool City Centre could well do without, at the present time, it is the motor bus (as it was originally called, to distinguish it from the horse bus). The centre of our city is full of them as they arrive, not in ones or twos, but often in double figures. There is a very real problem which has been exacerbated by the famous (or infamous) Deregistration Law, which permits market forces to prevail (at a dreadful cost to our health). As a result, a plethora of bus companies ply for custom in a slowly-choking city. The resulting air pollution can only be a serious danger to health, and how all these bus companies remain viable is a mystery.

However, it was not always so. In the writer's schooldays, Ribble, Crosville and the "Corpy" (the Corporation) buses served the city and suburbs – and served them well. Yet, in the late thirties, when the writer had to travel from Aintree to Crosby by bus to get to school, trams were still more popular. A statistic for 1934 shows a great difference in outlook (and therefore in policy) between Liverpool, Birkenhead and Wallasey. In Liverpool, buses were few and trams were much preferred. In Birkenhead, buses were plentiful while trams were fewer. Buses had driven trams off the streets in Wallasey. Financially, Liverpool buses could not compete against trams, but in Wallasey and Birkenhead buses showed a profit.

The history of the slow introduction of buses into Liverpool is well covered in several reference books in the LRO. If the reader's taste is for the details of the various fleets introduced, then he or she could do no better than dip into Paul Kelly's book *Liverpool's Buses* (Library reference number: Hq 388.406542753- KEL); or A.M.Witton's *Motor Buses* (Ref.no: H 338. 3 – WIT).

Claims to any Firsts, however, seem to be in short supply. The first to emerge was, that **the Liverpool bus service was the costliest in the country to run** – a claim we could well do without! The next concerned Wallasey which claimed to be **the first town in the world to have introduced the Leyland *Atlantean* double-decker buses.** These giants of the road, with their rear engines, their 78 seats and their front-entrance facility changed the face of British public transport. There may be a First in Liverpool's early preference for (if not love affair with) the original six-wheeler single-deckers that numbered 145 out of a total bus fleet of 171. From the takeover of a small company fleet of buses in 1911 until well after WW2, buses played second fiddle to trams.

The Mersey Tunnels

A road tunnel beneath the Mersey was first proposed as early as 1825. It was probably inspired by the creation of the Thames Tunnel Company in 1824 which wanted Brunel to drive a tunnel under the Thames from Rotherhithe to Wapping, using a tunnelling shield he had invented. About this time, Brunel visited Liverpool Docks and submitted a design for our **first floating landing stage.** Perhaps, while he was here, he also sowed the idea of a Mersey Road Tunnel. Unfortunately, the great upsurge of interest in railways eclipsed any interest in an underwater road tunnel at that time, and we had to wait until 1934 for the first such tunnel.

Today, there are three tunnels under the Mersey, linking Liverpool and the Wirral:

¤   The Mersey Railway Tunnel, opened in 1836. (See: Railways)

¤   The first Mersey Road Tunnel – *Queensway* – opened in 1934.

¤   The second Mersey Road Tunnel – *Kingsway* – opened 1972.

The First Mersey Road Tunnel

The decision to undertake such a venture was indeed a courageous one, for the underlying geological formations were complex and not known in any great detail. It was known that the main rock was Bunter Sandstone (laid down some 250 million years ago, probably south of the Equator) but the fault lines running through this rock were a problem. However, it had become clear that the age of the motor car had arrived. The queues of cars waiting to cross the river on the old car ferries were becoming longer and longer, so the pressure was on to look to the future and plan for a tunnel. Otherwise, Liverpool's trade was going to be seriously retarded.

1920: A Co-ordinating Committee was set up and three engineers were consulted: Sir Basil Mott, Sir Maurice Fitzmaurice and Liverpool's John A. Brodie who were unanimously in favour of the project.

1925: (8th August) A Private Bill authorising the project received the Royal Assent. The Mersey Tunnel Joint Committee was set up, consisting of 10 Liverpool Corporation and 7 Birkenhead Corporation members.

1925: (16th December) HRH the Princess Royal switched on the power for the pneumatic drills, and so inaugurated "an undertaking without parallel in engineering history."

1934: (18th July) The Tunnel was opened. It was 2.13 miles long (from Old Haymarket, Liverpool to King's Square, Birkenhead), with a branch tunnel on each side of the river. The under-river section consisted of a concrete tube, 13 metres in diameter. The engineers were Sir Basil Mott and J.A. Brodie, while the Entrance portal and associated buildings were designed in Art Deco style by H.J. Rowse. When built, the first Mersey Road Tunnel (locally known as "the Old Tunnel") was **the longest underwater road tunnel in the world.**

In 1925, Winston Churchill (at the Treasury) had broken the deadlock of long argument (regarding Tunnel finances and viability) by agreeing to a capital contribution of £2,500,000 with tolls to be charged for a period of twenty years. This cost had risen to £7,723,000 by the time of completion, and the period of toll charges had risen to 40 years. It was opened by HM King George V and Queen Mary and named, appropriately, Queensway.

The Second Mersey Road Tunnel

By the late 1950s it was obvious that the traffic problem was worsening and a report was called for by the Tunnel Joint Committee. Mott, Hay and Anderson produced a report which opined that, by 1970, six lanes of traffic might be required! Altogether, eight schemes – six tunnels and two bridges – were considered.

1965: Mersey Tunnel (Liverpool / Wallasey) Act given Royal Assent.

1967: (January). After extensive geological soundings along the proposed route of the tunnel using a long series of boreholes and a continuous geological survey using a "sparker" (a high- powered echo sounder), a pilot tunnel was completed after twelve months work.

1967: A Further Parliamentary Bill was promoted for a duplicate two-lane tunnel alongside the Second Tunnel. This was approved in 1968.

1967: (April) A contract was let to a consortium comprised of Nuttall, Atkinson and Company (the tunnel) and Sir James McAlpine & Co Ltd (the approach roads). Edmund Nuttall Ltd. entered into a partnership with the American contractor, Guy F. Atkinson, in order to get the use of their boring machine which had been used in boring tunnels for the Mangla Dam on the River Indus in West Pakistan.

The method of boring was revolutionary in more senses than one for a special, giant, mechanical "mole", manufactured in America, was used. **It was the longest tunnel-boring machine in the world**, being 45ft (15 metres) long and weighing 350 tons. It had already successfully bored five tunnels, each 500metres (1,500ft) long and 12 metres (36ft 8ins) in excavated diameter (reduced by modification to 11 metres (33ft 11ins) for the Mersey Tunnel).

The Mangla Mole (as it came to be known) began work in December 1967. There was no vibration at the surface and the cutting was speedier than any other system, with directional guidance being provided by a laser beam. Hence, **the breakthrough from Wallasey into the Liverpool side was accomplished on 4th March 1970.**

The "new tunnel", as it is termed locally, has a road width of 8 metres (24ft) for two lanes of traffic in each tunnel. The internal diameter is 10 metres (31ft 7ins). The official length (portal to portal) is 1.5 miles. There are many more fascinating details given of both tunnels in a book produced by the Mersey Tunnel Joint Committee, entitled *The Story of an Undertaking, The Mersey Tunnels.*

CANALS

The Sankey Canal

The Sankey Canal (Enabling Act: February 1755) was opened in November 1758, and ran from Parr (near St Helens) to the Mersey. Later extensions were to Gerard's Bridge, to Blackbrook Basin and to Ravenhead. (*A Guide to the Industrial Heritage of Merseyside,* NWSIAH 1978, 2nd Edition, pp 8 – 9.) **It was the first major artificial inland waterway to be constructed in England since Roman times.**

This canal has long been regarded as the first true canal in Britain because "its channel is totally independent of the Sankey Brook which it parallels". It owed its existence to Liverpool's need for coal and for the economic need to break the monopoly of the Liverpool & Prescot Turnpike Trust which was supplying coal by road transport – at great expense. It was sponsored by the Common Council of Liverpool who appointed Henry Berry, Liverpool's Dock Engineer, to construct the canal. (Berry Street is named after him).

The account in the book cited above is well worth reading and is detailed enough for the original path of the canal to be traced. The canal was finally abandoned in 1955.

The Leeds and Liverpool Canal

The need for a canal to link the eastern side of the Pennines to the Port of Liverpool was realised in the mid-1770s. Yorkshire businessmen made the first moves, even to the extent of having a survey made. The Liverpool businessmen had their own ideas, so the opening phases of the project were somewhat fraught with irritating argument and unproductive competitiveness. As fuller accounts of this second War of the Roses are well documented (LRO), it is not proposed to detail them here.

Eventually, agreement was reached and the first sods were cut, in 1770, at Halsall, which stands on the Maghull – Southport road across Downholland Moss. The Liverpool – Wigan section opened in the late 1770s, and the cut was finally pushed through to Leeds in 1816. With a total length of 127 miles from Leeds to Liverpool, it is **Britain's longest canal,** and, as it rises by several sets of locks to cross the Pennines near the Eden Valley, it is also **Britain's highest canal.** Two tunnels exist -Gannow Tunnel, 559 metres and Foulridge Tunnel, 1640 metres – barges used to be "legged" through these tunnels.

Its original terminal basin, in Liverpool, was at Leeds Street, and the line of the canal in that area can still be seen by looking at the curving line of old warehouses and buildings on the north-west side of that street. The canal's most useful local feature, still in existence, was Stanley Locks which let the barges down some 55 feet to dock level. By enabling loaded barges to come alongside a sailing or steam ship and unload directly into the vessel, several middlemen (carters and storemen, for instance) were eliminated, thus cutting cargo-handling costs considerably. There was no direct link with the Mersey until 1846 when the Stanley Dock Branch was cut.

The huge Stanley Bonded Warehouse (tobacco and spirits), dated 1900, was **the biggest bonded warehouse in the world.** It is still in use for storing industrial alcohol. Rumour has it that there is a huge lake of rum in the basement, sufficient for 9 million bottles of rum per year. As one wag remarked, when informed of this phenomenon, "Well, Liverpool is well known for the great spirit amongst its people."

AIRCRAFT & AIRPORTS

The citizens of Liverpool might well be expected to have nothing but loathing for aircraft – and could be forgiven for it – if one recalls the terror created by the hundreds of enemy aircraft that pulverised the city in the infamous May Blitz (mainly *Heinkel* 111s and *Junkers* 88s). Yet the turn-out for air displays, since the War, gives the lie to that view. The fact that 14 Squadrons of our own Fighter Aircraft fought in the skies over Liverpool perhaps restored the balance. The sight of American *Mustangs, Thunderbolts* and others, being shipped to Speke Airport from the docks through our streets, was one of the most heartening sights of the War as D-Day approached. (The Port, in fact, gained yet another First by **shipping in the greatest tonnage of war supplies of any port in the UK.**)

Yet we have had a long interest in aircraft and airports. It is not generally known, for instance, that Aintree Race Course was the first airport in Liverpool. During the **1914** War, aircraft parts (fuselage, wings, engines, etc.) were shipped into Aintree from the manufacturers and assembled there. Later, they were flown to the squadrons in the South of England for onward flights to northern France.

Hooton Park

Across the River Mersey at Hooton Park there was also a WW1 aerodrome, created in 1917 to train Royal Flying Corps pilots, until 1919. This fell into disuse until 1929 when a band of enthusiasts formed the Liverpool and District Aero Club, using the old airfield (grass) and its very substantial hangars, with planes generously donated by local public men. The club rapidly rose in importance to become the most active flying club outside London, with some spectacular successes:

¤   **national centre for light aircraft,**

¤   **centre for the popular aviation movement of the time,**

¤   many famous flights made to the ends of the Empire, and several records created,

¤   local air races and derbies organised,

¤   a staging post for the famous King's Cup national air races of the 1930s,

¤   **home of the famous Comper Aircraft Co., which produced the Comper CLA 7 *Swift*,**

¤   home for the Pobjoy Aeromotor Company which produced the **finest light aircraft 7-cylinder radial engines ever made**,

¤   visited in the late twenties and early thirties by many famous flyers, including Amy Johnson (lost over the Thames estuary while returning from a secret mission to France in WW2) and Sir Alan Cobham and his Flying Circus.

For a short time **Hooton Park was the only commercial aerodrome in the North of England**, preceding Speke (Liverpool) and Ringway (Manchester).

1930: Hooton officially became Liverpool Airport, until Speke took over in 1933.

1936: No.610 (County of Chester) Squadron, Royal Auxiliary Airforce, formed at Hooton – and served with honours in the Battle of Britain – 'The Few'.

WW2: Hooton was used by Coastal Command, operating flights over the Irish Sea from South Wales to Cumbria and also used for the assembly and repair of RAF aircraft by Messrs. Martin Hearn Ltd – a company founded on the site, in the mid-30s, by a former wing-walker from Cobham's Flying Circus.

Post-War: Aircraft assembly and repair continued until the mid-fifties when this service was extended to military and civil operators. In its final three years, Hooton was home to a reformed 610 Squadron, flying Gloster *Meteor* jet fighters, plus two other Auxiliary Air Force Squadrons.

1957: Hooton closed down.

1962: The airport was bought by Vauxhall Motors. Hooton had one thing in common with the Aintree aeroplane base – both were sited on race-courses.

Speke Airport

1928: Sir Alan Cobham helped to choose Speke as the site for the future airport. It is one of Fate's quirks that "Speke" comes from Old English "Spik", meaning "pig fields". (A new origin for the phrase, "pigs might fly" – as suggested by one wag?) Hooton, across the Mersey from Speke, had been considered, and there had also been talk of creating an airport behind The Bluebell pub at Huyton.

1930: (16th June) Official opening of flights to London (Croydon), via Manchester and Birmingham, from Speke Airport.

1933: (1 July) Official opening of Speke Airport by the Marquess of Salisbury, Secretary of State for Air. Liverpool became **the first provincial airport in the country.** On the opening day, the **biggest air show outside London** was presented, and 100,000 people from Merseyside attended. The classic photograph of the first Liverpool Airport shows a De Havilland *Dragon Rapide* aircraft standing outside a large farmhouse. The roof of the house had been opened up to house a large dormer-windowed room which was the control tower. A big letter *C* (for Control Tower) over this window ensured that visiting pilots knew where to park their aircraft.

The airlines of the day included: Imperial Airways, Aer Lingus, KLM, Railway Air Services, British Airways (the old company), Midland, and Scottish Air Ferries.

1934: First flight from a regional airport to Europe.

"*Dragon Rapide*" in front of the control tower at Speke

1936: The first hangar was built. The new airport building (based on the design of Munich Airport) was opened at this time. (It is now a Grade 2 listed building.)

WW2: *Spitfire* and *Hurricane* squadrons were housed on the airfield for the defence of Liverpool. Part of the property housed Rootes Factory (the first of the Shadow Factories?) where large numbers of Blenheims and Halifaxes were built, as well as Lockheed aircraft re-assembled from crates shipped over from the States.

An interesting First was the "special" unit called the **Merchant Ship Fighter Unit** which taught RAF fighter pilots to perform rocket-assisted take-offs from short metal ramps. Hurricanes were the chosen aircraft. Later, these pilots flew Hurricanes off similar ramps mounted in the bows of merchantmen in the Atlantic convoys. If, for instance, a German Focke-Wulf *Condor* was seen shadowing the convoy, the Hurricane was rocket-assisted off the merchantman for a one-way flight. The idea was to dispose of the enemy reconnaissance plane then crash-land in the sea near the parent ship, unless land was within range, which was a rare luxury. The loss of one Hurricane (the pilot usually landed near enough to a ship to be saved) was considered a fair exchange for the loss of a big German bomber with its crew of several expensively-trained airmen.

A Hurricane leaving a ship-launched fighter unit at Speke Airport

1950: (1st June) **First scheduled passenger helicopter service in Britain, from Speke to Cardiff via Wrexham.** Sadly, it did not prove economically viable.

1966: (7th May) New (Southern) runway opened by Prince Philip – the **longest provincial runway in the country.** The big mistake made was that no terminal building was built alongside the runway. This was possibly the main reason for our losing ground in the fight for the Liverpool Airport, versus Manchester. The fight for more traffic, and therefore a bigger airport, continues. Its present length is 8,200 feet, and it can handle the world's biggest aircraft.

1990s: Liverpool Airport (its correct title today) became **the first airport to move into the private sector.** It is owned by British Aerospace which has a 76 per cent shareholding. (Data kindly supplied by Mr Robin Tudor, Commercial Manager, Liverpool Airport.)

Flying Boats on the Mersey

1930s: Experiments were made to assess the viability of the Upper Pool of the Mersey (opposite Garston) as a seaplane base. The 1936 One Inch O.S. Map shows a seaplane base at Rock Ferry. Nothing came of this interest –

The flying-boat
'Caledonia'
which inaugurated
the trans-Atlantic
air service in 1937.
It made the cros-
sing in 14 hours

A Caledonia flying boat, perhaps used in the Mersey experiments

perhaps because of the weather pattern for this area which can be intimi-
dating or even lethal, especially over the upper Mersey Estuary.

FERRIES

Liverpool and the ferries go together because there has been a long love affair
between the people and the boats. It is to the everlasting shame of successive
governments that little or nothing has been done by them to ensure the
continued existence of the historic Mersey Ferries. There are very strong
social and even stronger historical reasons for such preservation. (We are
now down to using two ships out of our remaining three for the daily
schedules). But let us go back to the beginning.

1125: Benedictine monks at Birkenhead Priory established a ferry service
using large rowing boats. Passengers were often carried ashore by the
ferryman. The service was free because the rule of the Benedictine Order
was Charity – even to the extent of accommodating passengers in the Priory
(free) if the weather was too inclement for a crossing by open boat, which
was, and is, a frequent hazard.

A Charter granted by Edward III in 1320 allowed charges to be made.
Undoubtedly, the sigh of relief from the Priory's inhabitants may well have
constituted a First for the Order!

Henry VIII confiscated the ferries and privatised them by selling them to Thomas Worsley. They had various owners until finally taken over, last century, by the local Corporations on Merseyside – Birkenhead Ferries (with a red funnel) and Wallasey Ferries (white funnel). Today, as Mersey Ferries, they are part of Merseytravel. Again, the reader is urged to consult one of the many books written on the subject which can be found in our libraries and Record Office.

A few items make a legitimate claim for being Firsts. The *Royal Iris* and the *Royal Daffodil* come readily to mind. They were honoured with the "Royal" prefix by King George V after their heroic work in the 1914-16 War when **they led a successful operation to close the port of Zeebrugge to the Germans**. The funnel of the *Royal Daffodil*, riddled with bullet and shrapnel holes, stood for years (even after WW2) at the side of Seacombe Ferry.

A further claim for a First has already been mentioned (See: Port Radar) – namely, **the first ferry in the world to install a Radar system for safe navigation in fog.** The radar scanner may still be seen on top of the Seacombe Ferry Terminal clock tower.

It is interesting to note that at Woodside Ferry, at the top of each metal post holding up the gangways, there is a royal crown – because the ferries are a royal highway (from Woodside). Perhaps, some day, our "royal road" might be included in the Civil List!

THE UNIVERSITY

The term **"red-brick university" was first coined by one of the Liverpool University dons about 1943** (according to the *Daily Post*, 4th August 1969). The phrase was inspired by the blood-red brickwork of the first University Building on Brownlow Hill – the architectural trademark of the local architect, Alfred Waterhouse. He designed this building (including the Victoria Building with its impressive Tower), the old Royal Hospital (behind the University), and the Prudential Insurance Building in Dale Street, all in the same style. Because of his proclivity for blood- red brick, he was given the nickname "Slaughterhouse" Waterhouse by his architectural colleagues.

However, the campus also contains some very fine Georgian features, especially Abercrombie Square. This is a typical Georgian square with a little central park surrounded by gracious Georgian terraced houses. The square houses many of the university faculties including the Faculty of History, a delightful Art Gallery, and a building (Number 16) that was firstly the Confederate HQ in the American Civil War for the Confederate Consul in Liverpool, Mr Prioleau, then became the Bishop's Palace when the new Diocese of Liverpool was created in 1880, and currently is the University School of Education.

Where Senate House now stands once stood Foster's Georgian Church of St Catherine (1831) to complete the square. Just off the square, at the south-east corner, is a beautiful Regency church, recently refurbished at a cost of £2million. Once again, only a personal visit (preferably on a sunny day) will reveal the sheer joy of being in such beautiful surroundings, and a camera is strongly recommended for visitors to this highly photogenic place.

The Victorian era is well represented, with Waterhouse's Victoria Clock Tower (the gift of William Pickles Hartley, the Aintree jam manufacturer) and Building, several faculty buildings in the main quadrangles, and the Royal Hospital behind the quadrangle.

Liverpool University can claim many Firsts:

1892: The **Marine Biological Station** in Port Erin, IOM, was the **first such station belonging to a University**. Among other maritime achievements the Station made the University **the principal authority on seaweed.**

1904: The **first University in Britain to establish a School of Veterinary Science.** This led to the opening of the **first Veterinary hospital in the country in 1929**. Veterinary Science became a Faculty at the University in 1952.

1908: The first British University to establish a Professorship of Russian.

1909: The first Department of Civic Design (see below).

1919: The first University to have a Department of Oceanography.

Liverpool University School of Architecture

The first University School of Architecture in Britain was opened in 1895, and largely owed its existence to the success of a libel action brought by William Hesketh Lever (later, Lord Leverhulme) against a newspaper – an action in which Edgar Wallace, the crime novelist, was involved.

It seems that much was made by the plaintiffs of Edgar Wallace's report of an anonymous widow who supported her large family by taking in washing. She claimed that an increase in the price of soap was costing her 1s 6d weekly. There was laughter in court when Lord Leverhulme's counsel pointed out that the increased cost was so fractional, that to be affected to the extent of 1s 6d per week, the widowed washerwoman would have had to use 96 threepenny tablets of soap a week!

Lord Leverhulme, at the suggestion of the then Head of the **Bluecoat School**, spent £24,000 (almost half the libel proceeds) on buying Bluecoat Chambers as a home for student architects.

Department of Civic Design

Liverpool University was the first to establish a Department of Civic Design, in 1909, when Lord Leverhulme endowed a Chair. Further, the Department began publishing *The Town Planning Review* which is **the leading English-language journal on the subject.**

(For other Firsts at the University, see the 'Health' and 'Science and Technology' section.)

Index

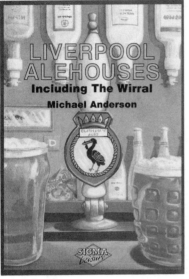

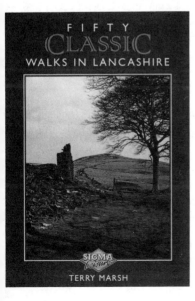

LIVERPOOL ALEHOUSES: including the Wirral

There must be more traditional pubs per square mile in Merseyside than anywhere in Britain - read about the pick of the crop in Michael Anderson's book - "...delightful...a notable work...a job well done" HOME BREW. *£6.95*

EAST LANCASHIRE WALKS

"East Lancashire Walks" is the companion volume to Reverend Smout's "West Lancashire Walks". The twenty routes cover the lowland area west of the Pennines, between Blackburn in the north and Warrington in the south. None is more than six miles in length. If you're an inhabitant of Liverpool, Manchester, Preston or Bolton you might not be aware of the haunted house near Warrington, or the American wood at Aspul, or the giant on the banks of the Mersey! *£6.95*

50 CLASSIC WALKS IN LANCASHIRE

This sequel to "50 Classic Walks in the Pennines" takes walkers through the much neglected, and far-reaching, county of Lancashire. There are many fine expanses of good walking country and places of beauty within the county's boundaries - known to the locals but waiting to be discovered by the wider population. With a map to accompany each walk, his own photographs and a comprehensive index, Terry Marsh again shares his vast experience. *£8.95*

BEST PUB WALKS IN LANCASHIRE

Neil Coates writes about Lancashire's rich pub heritage and a surprising variety of countryside for invigorating walks. This is the most comprehensive guidebook of its type. £6.95

TEA SHOP WALKS IN LANCASHIRE

Clive Price's selection of 30 walks through Lancashire - taking in the best tea-rooms on the way - is a must for all locals and visitors to the county. From flagged floors to luxurious carpets, from a Medieval barn to a working Post Office, the tea shops really are something special - and you can be sure the food is as good as the setting! The routes vary in length from 4 to 10 miles, so are suitable for all the family. They encompass lush riverside pastures and high, open moorlands and one enjoys the centre of Lancaster itself, with its ancient castle and Priory Church. As you explore both town and country, you can be sure of the reward of a delicious afternoon tea on the way! £6.95

CHILLING TRUE TALES OF OLD LANCASHIRE

Set in Victorian Lancashire, here is a spine-chilling collection of tales from Northern crime writer Keith Johnson - "...sure to thrill, chill and amaze" THE LANCASTER GUARDIAN. £6.95

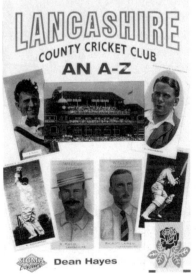